MANAGING THE FLEXIBLE WORKFORCE

Also available from Cassell:

Cox: *An Introduction to Office Management for Secretaries*
Davis: *Successful Advertising: Key Alternative Approaches*
Gatiss: *Total Quality Management*
Maitland: *Recruiting: How To Do It*
Morris: *Health and Safety: A Guide for the Newly Appointed*
Robson: *Essential Accounting for Managers*
Simons and Naylor-Stables: *Effective Communication for Managers*
Spencer and Pruss: *The Professional Secretary, Volumes 1 and 2*

Managing the Flexible Workforce

Richard Pettinger

CASSELL
London and Washington

Cassell
Wellington House
125 Strand
London WC2R 0BB

PO Box 605
Herndon
VA 20172

First published 1998

British Library Cataloguing-in-Publication Data
A catalogue record for this book is available from the British Library.

ISBN 0-304-70108-4 (hardback)
    0-304-70109-2 (paperback)

Designed and typeset by Kenneth Burnley at Irby, Wirral, Cheshire.
Printed and bound in Great Britain by Redwood Books, Trowbridge, Wilts.

Contents

List of summary boxes
and figures

Figures

Preface

Everywhere in the world there is a revolution going on, a transformation of business and of the services needed and wanted by people. There is a realization that, however organizational activities were organized and conducted in the past, new ways and better methods are essential for the future. Above all, this means a better understanding of the nature of work; the needs of all organizations to get the most from their resources – including their people; and to devise work methods and working patterns which fit into all of this.

Ever-greater strains and demands are placed on finite and diminishing resources. These therefore have to be arranged, planned, ordered and organized to ensure that they are used to greatest possible advantage. There is therefore a constant drive for improvement in efficiency and effectiveness in work activities. Structured, orderly, hierarchical types of organization are increasingly seen as a constraint on successful activities.

The drive is towards flexibility, dynamism, responsiveness – qualities which lead to increased levels of customer service. This is brought about by changing levels of customer expectations, much of which has happened as the result of improvement in product quality and levels of service as the result of technological advances and the successful activities of the industries of the Far East. In terms of public services, resource pressures are a real problem and this is certain to continue for the foreseeable future.

Flexible approaches to work are designed to address these issues. At their heart lies the need of organizations to maintain long-term existence, success, profitability and effectiveness in a rapidly changing and turbulent world. The best way to do this, is to ensure that the people concerned – the staff – have the necessary skills, qualities, attitudes and approaches to work. From an organizational point of view, this means attention to the demands of its own particular customers and creating work methods and patterns that are suitable.

After all, flexible working in itself is not new. Health, energy and transport services have always had to be available 24 hours a day, seven days a week, all year round, to meet the needs of those using them. Unconventional and irregular patterns of work have therefore existed for a very long time. Multinational companies locating in different parts of the world have had to adjust their methods of work to take account of local customs and pressures; and to train and re-train local and indigenous workforces so that the work is carried out effectively within these constraints.

Small and medium-sized enterprises have long had to adopt flexibility as an attitude.

Whether in responding to one-off requests or producing specialist items, their very existence has always depended on producing customer and client satisfaction in these circumstances.

Consultancies and agencies have to work on the premise that each new problem, request or issue that comes into them will be unique, different, specialized and have its own particular set of circumstances. Again therefore, it has always been necessary to adapt particular expertise to changing sets of circumstances so that an effective – and profitable – response is always given.

The drive for flexibility – and dynamism and responsiveness – is therefore based on a combination of that which exists already, and the potential for future development and improvement. Part of this relates to ever more detailed attention to costs and investment, and the need to gain the best value and returns on each; the other side of the coin is the need to engage corporate and managerial attitudes, the chief of which is an understanding and acknowledgement of the fact that there are specific types of investment, and specific skills and expertise, that are needed in flexible working situations.

This is the standpoint taken in this book. Its purpose is to cover the main issues that have to be faced. Chapter 1 is a description of the general approach to flexible working and an indication of the context and organizational approach necessary if it is to be successful. Chapter 2 is a description and analysis of specific flexible work patterns and the advantages and disadvantages of using particular forms of employment. Chapter 3 covers the contractual arrangements that have to be faced. Chapter 4 is a study of motivating and rewarding the flexible workforce, and of the obligations and issues that have to be faced by individuals working under flexible arrangements, and those who manage them. Chapter 5 is a detailed discussion of the human resource management arrangements that have to be in place. Chapter 6 covers in detail the different managerial aspects of arranging, planning, co-ordinating and controlling flexible working; and the necessity for high quality staff and management training. Chapter 7 draws all the different threads together; and is illustrated with examples from different organizations that have adopted flexible working attitudes and practices in their own ways.

There are three Appendices. Appendix A is a detailed briefing on UK employment law indicating the range of features and elements of which those engaging in flexible working need to be aware. Appendix B is a copy of the European Community Social Charter which indicates the extent of European influences on UK employment practice. Appendix C is a glossary of technical terms used.

Chapter 1

Introduction

Flexible working is the term used to describe the creation of work patterns and arrangements based on the need to maximize and optimize organizational output, customer satisfaction and staff expertise and effectiveness. It has come about as the result of the expansion of globalization of competition and choice, increased pressures on all resources, enhanced customer demands and expectations, and changes in patterns of consumption.

Flexible workforces are created to maximize and optimize the use of capital, premises, technology and equipment, to produce high quality products and services that are available to customers where and when required.

Flexible working is not new. Energy, telecommunications, emergency services, health care, transport, travel and leisure services have always operated around the clock. Personal selling – of insurance, building products, double glazing – has always taken place at times suitable to customers, especially evenings and weekends. Since the middle of the 1980s much of this has been extended into retail, banking and some office services.

Flexible work and extended working hours have therefore been around for a long time. The purpose here is to consider the potential, the opportunities, and also the pitfalls, afforded by flexible working in order to ensure that organizations that follow this path gain the best results possible, identify the best approaches, and avoid the main problems.

The flexible workforce is a combination of:

FLEXIBLE WORKFORCE

- patterns of work, based on hours, expertise, needs and demands of customers and clients, the capability and capacity of technology, location and specific aspects of particular activities;
- attitudes and values, especially responsibility, dynamism, individual and collective responsiveness, commitments to service and satisfaction, positive approaches to solving problems;
- a commitment to training and development, enhancing the value brought by all members of staff to the organization;
- individual and collective commitment to improve all aspects of work,

procedures, practices, response times as well as products and services;
- organizational commitment to flexibility and to each of the above points, and a commitment to invest in and support everything that is necessary to achieve this (see Summary Box 1.1).

SUMMARY BOX 1.1

The NatWest Tower, Bishop's Gate, London EC1

The NatWest Tower is the headquarters of the National Westminster Bank. It was designed and built in 1981 as a high profile, high prestige symbol of the Bank's enduring quality and continuing affluence.

In a study carried out in 1996 by the Bartlett School of Architecture, Building, Design and Town & Country Planning, University College, London, it was found that:

- on a series of random sampling activities carried out over a three-month period, the Tower was on average only 33% occupied;
- on one occasion, the Tower was only 15% occupied.

There is clearly a strong cultural and perceived commercial pressure to have such premises. However, this has to be balanced against the fact that on the basis of this study, a great deal of capital is being tied up in facilities which (rationally) are not being used to full advantage.

This also has to be balanced against the real and perceived advantages of giving people their own specific space and territory. In some cases the commercial and operational advantage that accrues from having a fully equipped specified location available for predetermined business activities clearly outweighs the cost of otherwise having the space empty.

At the very least, the example indicates the need for constant monitoring and review of space and facilities utilization.

Flexibility

Flexibility is a corporate attitude; and the flexible workforce is the product of this corporate attitude. The reasons for having a flexible workforce are:

- to produce better quality, more effective work;
- to develop the reservoir of talent and potential that exists in all workforces, and which traditionally has remained constricted by procedures and hierarchies or otherwise largely untapped;
- to serve customers and clients at times suitable to them. This is especially true of retail and other service activities, following the decision of supermarkets, agencies, restaurants and other shops to open for longer hours, and following the Sunday Trading Act of 1992 which further extended their scope for opening;
- to make full use of talented persons who (for a variety of reasons) are unable to work regular or traditional patterns or hours, and to harmonize their capabilities with the demands of customers and the requirements of organizations (see Summary Box 1.2).

The affluent worker

The 'Affluent Worker' studies were carried out in the late 1950s at Luton, Bedfordshire. The purpose of the studies was to ascertain levels of motivation and morale among the workforce. It also dealt in some detail with alienation, identity and the loyalty of the workforce to the company.

Three companies were studied in detail – Laport Chemicals; Skefco Ball Bearings Ltd; and Vauxhall, the car makers. At each company, work was highly specialized. Members of the workforce were given very specific jobs to do. They were not normally allowed to exceed these jobs. Supervision was distant and coercive. The main problems that were found concerned boredom, repetition and a complete lack of willingness to take any direct interest in the company products or state of well-being. There was also a general indication that this form of work led to serious mental and physical health problems (and this has subsequently been strongly demonstrated in more recent studies).

The companies studied paid their staff extremely well. However, high levels of payment did not compensate for the levels of boredom or alienation experienced. Nor did this in any way alleviate the health problems indicated.

Moreover, these practices have not lasted. Each company has since transformed all of their work practices and arrangements. Those working on production processes are now fully skilled and transferable between departments and activities. At Laport and Vauxhall, staff training is not optional. At Vauxhall also, there are moves afoot (not yet fully realized) to make specific production teams responsible for quality assurance and customer complaints on the cars and car products produced on their particular line.

Vauxhall especially suffered severe industrial relations problems over the entire post-war period up to 1979; and there have been less serious disputes in 1983, 1989, 1991 and 1996. One of the findings of the 'Affluent Worker' studies was that the strike/industrial dispute was a tool available for the use of both workforce and management. Above all, it could be used as a safety valve by either party when the pressures inherent in this kind of working built up to intolerable levels. This approach to strikes and other industrial activity has subsequently been found to have been extensively used in all mass production and primary activities over the period 1945–1985.

Part of the transformation of this form of activity – in both these and other companies – has been to engender the qualities and attitudes inherent in the flexible approach. In the main, this has concentrated on staff training and development, multi-skilling and job enlargement. Alongside this however, there is plenty of evidence to suggest that the required attitudes have also been developed – and this is borne out by the evidence of the level of dispute at Vauxhall in 1991 and 1996. Both disputes arose simply as the result of misunderstandings over pay awards and working arrangements; rather than being allowed to fester (or being used actively as a release), they were settled very quickly.

Key qualities

For effective flexible work to take place, the following must be present:

- *Staff commitment:* to the organization, its customers, clients, products and services; to the quality of whatever is offered; to customer satisfaction and contentment; to continuous personal and occupational development and advancement.
- *Organizational commitment:* to its staff, to products, its services, its customers and clients; to improvement in all areas and activities, including the quality of management and administration; to continuous training and development to improve the capabilities and expertise of the workforce.
- *Dynamism and responsiveness:* rather than passiveness and dependency on procedures and bureaucracy.
- *Empathy:* with customers and clients; with managements and supervision; with peers, superiors and subordinates; with suppliers and distributors; with governors, shareholders and backers.
- *Identity:* between the organization and its staff; between the organization and its customers and clients; within immediate work teams; with its wider environment and community; and with others with whom the individual comes into contact.

This is underpinned by the creation and development of positive attitudes and values in all areas. The responsibility for this rests entirely with the organization. None of this can take place without organizational commitment. Flexibility and capability in skills, knowledge, attitude, behaviour and expertise all feed off each other. It all leads to greater all-round understanding, capability and confidence, and to the required levels of commitment.

Expectations

Flexible attitudes and approaches to work raise the expectations of everyone. Shareholders, governors and directors of organizations expect increased levels of efficiency, effectiveness, profitability, all-round performance and all that entails – improved morale, increased sales and levels of service, increased customer satisfaction, reduced levels of complaints, better and fuller use of technology and equipment and higher returns on investment.

Staff expect an increased job interest and satisfaction, work variety, opportunities for training, development and advancement and higher pay and reward levels. They anticipate greater feelings of identity. By virtue of being multi-skilled, they expect greater job and employment security. They expect to be redeployed rather than made redundant when one set of activities comes to an end. They expect to be consulted on work methods and patterns, form levels of performance, to know what is going well and why, and what could be improved.

Customers expect product quality and service levels to be maintained and improved. They expect to be valued. They anticipate a long and beneficial relationship. Because of the increases in competition and choice, they are entitled to expect these high levels of quality and service; and organizations must anticipate that customers will look elsewhere for satisfaction if this is not forthcoming or if levels and quality fall.

Pitfalls

There are potential problems in raising the expectations of everyone concerned and then not being able to meet them. Successful flexible working therefore arises as the result of a strategic decision that this is the best way forward for the particular organization, department or division. It consists of:

- a long-term commitment to creating the necessary environment and conditions supported and resourced by top management;
- investment in up-to-date technology, staff training and development, and organization development;
- a long-term view of the results desired. These do not happen overnight and the benefits may not be apparent for months, or even years (see Summary Box 1.3);

SUMMARY BOX 1.3

Short-termism

Short-termism is the anticipation and expectation of instant or near instant results. There are great stakeholder pressures for this. Shareholders expect annual results that produce dividends on their shares. In public services, governors and budget holders expect financial targets to be met so that they meet the aspirations of politicians; in extreme cases, this (rather than the service demand) is the overriding driving force. Media analysts, financial journalists and consultants expect instant results and returns as they have to make instant pronouncements about companies and organizations.

Short-termism is therefore highly influential and a major driving force in many circumstances. It is also self-evidently in direct contrast to required and sustainable levels of business activity. Neither business nor public service activities cease on the date of the annual report only to start up again the following day. The example of Japanese companies locating in the West is also in direct contrast to this approach – without exception these companies have taken the view that, as they have come to locate permanently, their first duty is to provide permanent employment and permanent high quality products.

Moreover, as an attitude, flexibility requires a long-term and sustainable commitment if it is to become a reality. Instant results are not therefore apparent as the result of 'adopting' a 'culture' of flexibility. Short-term minor achievements may become apparent. The full benefits of flexible working – technology maximization, the optimization/maximization of customer access and the employment of high quality, fully motivated staff – only become apparent over the long term.

- a long-term commitment to creating the required skills, knowledge, attitudes, behaviour and expertise; including training programmes, job rotation, enlargement and enrichment; opportunities for project work and secondments; development of potential for the future: drawing out talents and capabilities of everyone; identifying their strengths and weaknesses and maximizing the use of strengths;
- a commitment to organizational performance based on the long-term view rather than the pursuit of instant or short-term results. Again, this requires continuous and substantial investment in training and development, technology, attention to work methods, procedures and practices, an attitude of continuous improvement of everything in and around the workplace; all of which is conducted in the pursuit of customer satisfaction;
- a commitment to supporting staff, supervisors and managers in their decisions and activities.

CONCLUSIONS Flexible working is a form of organizational investment, the purpose of which is getting the best out of existing and finite resources, especially the workforce. It is only successful and effective if organizations and their top managers:

- take a long-term view – the creation of a flexible workforce requires time and resources, training and development, attention to work division and job descriptions, and attention to pay and rewards;
- reappraise and realign the duties and priorities of their middle managers and supervisors towards maximizing and optimizing staff performance and customer satisfaction, and away from short-term results and the operation of procedures and systems;
- streamline and simplify administrative procedures and systems in order to concentrate on primary performance, attitudes and behaviour and resolving (rather than institutionalizing) problems;
- realign their own priorities, objectives and targets in support of this.

Flexible working is not cheap. Some cost savings may be possible in some circumstances. For example, corporate accommodation costs can often be cut where people are employed in working from home. This may, in some circumstances, be extended to the removal of administrative activities and some forms of supervision

Above all, flexible working requires long-term commitment. It stems from organizational policy and strategy. Only when that is clear can attention usefully and effectively be paid to:

- hours and patterns of work;
- contractual arrangements and implications;
- organization development and improvement;
- the nature and level of investment;
- managing and developing the flexible workforce;
- managing and developing flexible workforce management.

Chapter 2

Hours and patterns of work

INTRODUCTION   Flexible working is best seen in a broad context. This is as follows:

- careers and occupations that last 40 years, based on a 40-hour working week for 48 weeks of the year, are no longer viable; everyone (whatever their expertise or preference) must expect to experience great changes in occupation; the ways in which things are done; the obsolescence of some occupations and the creation of new ones;
- earnings levels no longer rise steadily, nor are they the product of a combination of loyalty, promotion, and enhanced expertise; people now tend to expect enhanced rewards today, rather than the promise of enhanced rewards tomorrow;
- core and peripheral activities, in which organizations increasingly structure their workforce according to the peaks and troughs of activities; drives towards contracting out specialist activities to specialist organizations rather than retaining expensive expertise in-house, especially when they are only occasionally required; the creation of networks that can be called upon at short notice to handle problems or cater for sudden upturns in activities;
- the extension of part-time and intermittent patterns of employment to cope with the peaks and troughs of business demand;
- the extension of activities covered by alternative patterns of employment, especially home-working and subcontracting;
- the nature of the organization's activities and the particular pressures and constraints that are present; production and operational pressures; any constraints placed by technology; the demands of customers and the nature of their relationship with the organization;
- the blurring of the distinction between full-time and part-time patterns of employment; in the UK there is now very little difference in basic employment rights between full-time and part-time staff, and it is normally best practice to treat them exactly the same (see also Chapter 3).

This is the context in which consideration of different patterns of employment and hours of work takes place. The overall drive is to synchronize employee working hours with operational demands. This has the purpose of having people present when they are needed, and not present when they are not needed. It reduces costs, improves the effectiveness of the human resource and ultimately improves organizational performance.

Whatever the hours worked, or nature of the job to be done, the following characteristics need to be satisfied:

WORK CONTENT

- people need to have some degree of autonomy over the way tasks are to be achieved; people should have a certain amount of responsibility for their own work, for the resources that they use and for the way in which they structure and organize their working day;
- variety should be present;
- repetitive tasks should be kept to a minimum;
- people should receive regular feedback on their performance, and this should be carried out face-to-face in the course of normal supervision;
- the place of the job in the wider scheme of things should be clearly understood;
- social contact should be available wherever practicable (see Summary Box 2.1);

SUMMARY BOX 2.1

Social contact

One of the great strengths of traditional methods of work organization is the high degree of social contact afforded. It is essential that this is provided in flexible (especially non-located) methods of working.

Much of this will be carried out by telephone. It is also necessary to arrange and schedule meetings between members of the flexible workforce, and at least a part of these meetings should be an opportunity for general social interaction. The rest of such meetings should be concerned with dealing with substantial work and organizational issues. The purpose of this approach is to ensure that at least a measure of substitution of the enduring and constant social interaction afforded by attending regularly at designated places of work is available.

In many cases, the ground is extremely well trodden and simply needs translating into other kinds of flexible working as and when they arise. For example, sales teams make arrangements to meet up regularly. In the transport industry, crews meet regularly. In the particular example of the UK railway industry, in the 1970s there was found to be a direct correlation between threats of industrial action by the train drivers and the frequency of staff meetings – where staff meetings were few and far between, union meetings became ever more militant and confrontational.

At this stage therefore, the purpose is to make sure that the principle of social contact and interaction is well understood by anyone who is contemplating flexible working for whatever purpose. This is part of the investment necessary in successful flexible working arrangements. While this should never be indulgent or wasteful, a measure of latitude is clearly necessary as part of the drive for effective and successful work and output.

- learning, training and development opportunities should be in-built into work patterns;
- people need to know what is expected of them in terms of performance, attitude, behaviour and demeanour;
- all people must be treated fairly and evenly at all times, whatever their occupation or pattern of work;
- work should have distinctive measures of success and failure; people should know and understand the means by which success and failure are evaluated.

From the employee's point of view therefore, the hours should be long enough and regular enough to enable a sufficient amount of work to be carried out to give feelings of satisfaction and achievement. The longer and more regular the hours, the quicker a real identity and commitment is generated. Where hours are short and intermittent, there is a pressure on managers and supervisors to take additional steps to build this identity and commitment quickly.

From the employer's point of view, the issue is the ability to integrate this with the frequency, regularity, length of work period that the employee is present and the output that is required, feasible or achievable. People on different hours and patterns of work have to be integrated with one another so that an effective working environment and relationship is created. The greater the ability to do this, the greater the reduction in the use and administration of procedures and problem-solving, thus freeing up time and resources for productive and profitable activities.

Whatever the nature or patterns of work, everyone works better in a clean, comfortable and wholesome environment. This does not mean luxury. Moreover, there are work pressures and constraints to be considered – especially where work is to be carried out in extremes of heat or cold, wet or dry, or in dangerous conditions. Within this context, it should normally be possible to provide everyone with basic standards of comfort and cleanliness; rest, refreshment and meal-time arrangements; car parking or transport to and from the workplace; and adequate standards of warmth and comfort. Making this available to everyone reinforces the value, respect and esteem in which everyone is held regardless of their pattern of work or length of working hours.

NOTE

It is true that in exceptional cases, a bad working environment leads to a Dunkirk spirit among the staff. It is much more usual however, for this to remain a point of contention and to become a real problem when other things go wrong. It is especially true for those who make only infrequent visits to the organization (for example, part-timers, field sales staff, home-workers); no one wants to go to a tatty, dirty or unkempt environment. People will tend to stay away as much as they possibly can and this reinforces, rather than breaks down, the barriers between them and their organization.

The main patterns are

- *Annual hours:* where the number of hours of work required each year of the employee is established and patterns of work agreed between the individual and the organization; in the UK the normal upper figure on this is 2,000 hours (which represents an equivalent of 40 hours per week for 50 weeks of the year).
- *Compressed working:* where 'full-time' hours are worked, but compressed into fewer working days – for example, instead of working eight hours a day for five days, people work ten hours per day for four days or even 12–15 hours per day for three days.
- *Term time working:* in which those with responsibilities for school-age children are either given extensive unpaid leave, or else required to take their annual leave during the school holidays.
- *Continental shifts:* whereby people follow patterns of work such as 4 days on and 2 days off, or 3 days on and 2 days off so that the whole week is covered in a fair manner.
- *Hours to suit:* where the demands of the work are reconciled with the work-time preferences of the employees.
- *Twilight shifts:* where work is offered between 5.30 pm and 10.30 pm to people (often married women, students and those of school age) enabling them to fit work around their other commitments.
- *Flexitime:* based on:
  - core periods, when attendance is compulsory, either for a given period every day, or for a given period on certain days;
  - optional time, which is attendance at other than core times, enabling employees to choose the time suitable to themselves when they are most productive; and again to reconcile this with their other demands and commitments.
- *Job sharing:* where a single position is shared out between two or more persons. Job sharing works best when the post is shared between two persons. For reasons of administration and control, it is both unusual and impractical to share the post between more than three persons (see Summary Box 2.2).

Long hours

On the face of it, having one member of staff working up to 60 hours per week and possibly taking work home in the evenings on their days off (or failing to take all their leave entitlement) is attractive, because a large return is being made on one salary. If there really is 60 hours worth of

Job sharing was originally devised in the UK in the late 1970s as a means by which persons with other responsibilities (above all, women with young families) could be encouraged back into the workforce. At the time, the advantages were seen as combining the need for regular full-time work with the other demands of the potential members of staff.

The principle of job sharing is well established in UK public services. School teaching, nursing and social work are all occupations in which designated full-time posts are shared between more than one (usually two) members of staff.

There are two main approaches. The first is whereby each member of staff works their designated proportion of the working week – for example, the first person works Monday, Tuesday and Wednesday morning, the second person works Wednesday afternoon, Thursday and Friday. The other method is whereby one person works mornings only and then hands over to the other person who works afternoons only. Wages and salaries are paid by the organization on a 50-50 split in the examples given. This varies if, for example, one person works three days and the other works two.

The main problem concerns work loading. It is a real problem if, for example, the two busiest days of the week are Thursday and Friday and that the job share is divided at Wednesday lunchtime. This also remains a problem if each person concerned is working a part of every day and a highly pressurized workload has to be handed over at lunchtime.

Job sharing is currently less of an attraction than it used to be. The reason for this is because it is now much easier to employ staff on hours and terms and conditions suitable both to the individual and to the organization rather than designating specific posts as full-time or part-time for which a job share may then become one option.

high quality work to be done each week, this can only be sustained by one person in the very short term. Over longer periods, the quality of work, personal health and personal life all suffer (see Summary Box 2.3).

This applies in most cases. Employees, often quite willingly, carry out overtime or work additional periods during their time off. The end result again is stress and burn-out. Moreover, the employee becomes disappointed, frustrated and angry when the overtime and extra shifts come to an end, as their standard of living then suffers.

Short hours

If hours are too short and intermittent, the employee has no opportunity to build up any true working relationship with colleagues, managers and supervisors, or with the organization. The result, again, is frustration and disappointment. This occurs even if for some reason employees have

There is a culture among managerial, professional and white collar staff in the UK of the work-based lifestyle. This consists of putting in long hours to demonstrate commitment, loyalty and dedication. In many cases, a proportion of social life becomes centred around work. Long hours are invariably necessary once in a while. If they are continually necessary, it is either because the job is too big for one person, or because the job holder is not capable of doing it.

The problem is exacerbated when organizations are seen or known to reward employees for putting in this form of long hours commitment. It is extremely prevalent in multinational company and public service headquarters activities. For example a major telecommunications corporation in 1994 provided all of its staff with bonuses and performance related pay awards based solely on the number of hours worked (rather than the quality of output achieved as the result). The group general manager of a large insurance market insists that he judges all of his staff by the time at which they arrive at work and the time at which they leave – again, with scant regard to the output achieved. One of the recently privatized UK rail companies insists that its drivers hold themselves at all times in readiness, either to work extended or double shifts in case of staff shortages or non-attendance.

In practice, this is a substitute for effective output. Insofar as there is an operational purpose, it is a vague notion only that the longer people are at work, the more likely it is that they will produce something that is effective. This is very different from views held elsewhere in the world – especially France where for example, the cultural stereotype is that if the job cannot be done in the designated hours of work, then the job holder is not competent to do it and should be replaced.

There is also a serious problem with this once the anticipated rewards do not materialize. Key, and otherwise effective, members of staff become demoralized and seek work elsewhere. In the short term, the perceived necessity of being at work for long hours may be very good for an individual's morale and self-esteem. In the medium to long term, this is not sustainable – and again, if the rewards are not forthcoming, the net result is to make the employee feel unvalued rather than valued, and disrespected rather than respected.

chosen their hours of work. Where short periods of work are required, where part-time is the normal employment pattern, hours should still be long and regular enough to build up a mutual identity and positive beneficial relationships.

Hours to suit

This should *only* be offered on the employer's terms alone, where the work permits this, or where there is otherwise no possibility of filling the vacancy. Problems arise especially where the employee picks odd hours on odd days where they perceive at the present that they may be free and available for work; if their circumstances change, so will their availability for work and this again leads to problems. Problems also arise where the employee chooses a general pattern of work that is too intermittent or too vague for them to build up any sense of identity or purpose with the organization – which is, after all, the purpose of the exercise. Something that may be attractive from an employee's point of view when they are designing their 'hours to suit' quickly becomes demoralizing for them when they realize that their level of involvement is not sufficient to gain any sort of identity. Invariably, they will not have known enough about this at the outset to make sure that their 'hours to suit' address the problem once they are in the organization.

Flexitime

Flexitime is attractive and popular with people, because it normally allows them to build up additional leave entitlement through the amount of hours that they work during the optional period. It is most commonly found in white collar and service sectors, and is increasingly being extended to production and sales functions (see Summary Box 2.4).

Job sharing

Problems with job sharing arise when, for some reason, it becomes impossible for the job sharers to continue to work together.

It may also be necessary to consider variations in work pressures – for example, where the job share splits the working week into mornings and afternoons, and where it is more stressful in the mornings; or where the working week is divided at Wednesday lunchtime and the work is more pressurized on Thursday and Friday than Monday and Tuesday.

NOTES

1   If additional hours are required, these should first be offered to existing staff. This is especially important where people are on patterns of low or infrequent attendance as it gives the opportunity to develop the total working relationship. This also reduces the need for unnecessary recruitment, selection, induction and job training, and the administrative burden that these create.

2   Those on distinctive patterns of employment – for example, Saturday and Sunday crews in retail; permanent night shifts – need the same positive identity and commitment to be generated as everyone else. Otherwise, these groups may become isolated and this tends to lead to unofficial work regulation and canteen cultures.

In the UK, there are two distinctive flexitime systems.

Core hours

These occur where the employee is required to be present for specific hours on specific days, ideally when work is at its heaviest or customer/client demand is at its most frequent. Beyond this, the employee is given the opportunity to choose how they make up the rest of their work commitment. This may be to come in very early in the morning so that work can be carried out before the organization gets into full swing; or the opportunity to work late into the evening so that work can be carried out after the organization has passed its peak loading.

Core days

This is where the organization requires attendance/work commitment on designated days for the forthcoming period. This may be because of specific contracts, commissions or customer pressures; or as a matter of organization policy. This especially applies to home-workers and others working away from the organization location. On these occasions, the employees are expected to make themselves available according to the demands of the organization. For the rest of the time, the workload is theirs to organize so that the output is achieved.

Whichever method is adopted, it is normal that a keying in, clocking in or logging system is used by the employee to confirm the hours or days of work carried out. As stated in the main text, one of the advantages to the employee of this approach is the ability to build up a sufficient bank of hours or days worked to entitle them to additional days off. It is unusual to give more than two days off per employee, per month, in return for working this way. If the scheme goes beyond this then attendance for over-long periods of time is encouraged and (see Summary Box 2.3 above) work output as well as morale and overall effectiveness all decline.

Whatever the hours agreed, the main issues are:

- to get the best possible work out of the member of staff;
- to gain a proper professional and committed working relationship;
- to give the member of staff the opportunity to earn a fair living;
- to build a positive and mutually productive continuing relationship.

Enrichment

Job and work enrichment has the purpose of making all work as satisfying and fulfilling as possible. It applies to any form of work that becomes mundane, repetitive or routine, all of which tend to lead to disaffection and boredom – and therefore loss of performance. It takes the following forms.

OTHER PATTERNS OF WORK

- *Rotation:* in which the employee is changed or rotated through a variety of tasks, activities and work stations. This should occur regularly enough to generate interest, but not so regularly as to fragment the work being carried out.
- *Enlargement:* in which the employee is given additional tasks and (increasingly) responsibilities attached to the main duties. Additional tasks often include quality control, customer liaison and dealing with problems and queries.
- *Consultation:* in order to get the employee's view of the best way of carrying out the work; on new work and work station design; choice of new equipment; problems with existing equipment.
- *Training and development:* for current activities; for the future; to identify potential and aptitudes; to pursue personal choices and preferences (see Figure 2.1), as well as organizational and occupational necessities.
- *Project work:* based on a combination of organizational requirements and personal drives. Much of this often stems from suggestion schemes and membership of work improvement groups and quality circles. Some of this may also arise from secondments and from the continuous need for fresh approaches to problems.

Enrichment builds on and reinforces positive attitudes and commitment. It strengthens the mutual identity and interest of employee and employer. It identifies personal potential and aptitudes, and enlarges the fund of talent and expertise available.

Figure 2.1

Training and development: the personal/ professional/ organization mix.

1. Implications and considerations (see also Fig. 5.4)

POSITIVE		NEGATIVE
Interest, fulfilment, preference	——— *PERSONAL* ———	Indulgent, wasteful, preferential
Ever-changing, ever-developing, CPD	——— *PROFESSIONAL OCCUPATIONAL* ———	Restraining, narrow, restricting, introspective
Securing the future	——— *ORGANIZATIONAL* ———	Specialized, narrow, for the present

Empowerment

Empowerment is a form of job enrichment which involves employees in any or all of the following:

- Taking on additional responsibility for administration, customer satisfaction, record keeping, cashing up (for example, in restaurants and checkout work).

- Taking on extra duties, e.g.: bank and retail cash desk and checkout staff, taking on sales and customer service functions.

- Being allowed to use initiative in acting in the organization's best interests in its dealings with its customers.

- Work improvement groups, quality improvement groups, quality circles which are given broad remits in which to work and allowed initiative and responsibility to carry out their tasks.

- Suggestion schemes, especially those which give employees scope, and sometimes a budget, to put their proposals into practice and which reward them for extra profits made or reductions in costs.

Apart from tackling specific problems and issues, these activities contribute to employee and organizational development and reinforce commitment to product quality and customer service (see Summary Box 2.5).

Home-working

Home-working is attractive all round. For the employer, there is no need to provide expensive production, operational or office space as that is the employee's home. For the employee, there is no need to travel to work. Home-working is well established in various sectors – for example, computer software, fashion and clothing sales, journalism, financial services, cosmetics. Its potential is limited only by the approach and the imagination of managers, and the attitudes of organizations and the strong demands of large sectors of the population that they physically separate their working and non-working lives. There is great potential for administration, financial management, purchasing and supply to be carried out by people working at work stations established in their own homes – and potential therefore for organizations to curtail their premises' requirements (see Summary Box 2.6).

Fixed-term arrangements

Fixed-term arrangements occur where people are taken on for a specific period of time to do a particular job; where there is a requirement for absence cover (e.g. maternity); and where people are taken on for the duration of a project, however long that lasts.

The boundaries are clearly stated in advance so that it is known to both employee and employer when the work is to finish.

A form of fixed-term arrangement is also often used for research jobs and to pursue ideas to see if they have potential. Employers normally place a deadline by which likely results should at least become apparent.

SUMMARY BOX 2.5

Sony and empowerment

The Sony Corporation of Japan was one of the first to take a broad approach to staff empowerment. It concentrated on the following:

- *Clocking on.* In 1971, procedures for clocking on were abolished. All staff were given the responsibility of turning up and starting work on time. At a stroke, this removed the need for time clocks, time clock cards and clerical staff responsible for calculating the precise hours that individuals had worked. It was assumed that people would turn up on time and that they would carry out the work for which they were responsible. The style of supervision adopted purely concerned itself with attendance problems (rather than according the fact of everybody's attendance). This approach also reduced the need for extensive coercive and confrontational forms of supervision.

- *Product quality.* The factory at Atsugi produced transistors and microprocessors. Again in 1971, the decision was taken to make all production staff responsible for the quality of their product. Customer complaints and queries would therefore be addressed directly to the person who had made the item rather than going through a quality assurance division. Again this reduced the need for additional staff as well as ensuring that the production personnel concentrated on quality as well as output.

- *Facilities management.* This was handed over to a small team of cleaners, security staff and maintenance personnel. They themselves negotiated the standards of cleanliness and quality of working environment directly with the rest of the members of the organization. The result again transferred responsibility from a coercive and confrontational form of management to everybody who worked at the factory. In turn, the result was that the Atsugi plant became a model of factory organization to which managers and also other staff from the other Japanese corporations came to visit and observe this form of management.

In summary, all of those matters with which more traditional forms of supervision were concerned on a daily basis were handed over directly to everybody concerned; and the result was that the quality of the working environment was something to which everybody subscribed. Any problems were dealt with on an individual basis. Only one specific problem was subsequently documented – graffiti in one block of toilets; and this was cleared up when one of the cleaning staff caught and confronted a group of people from elsewhere in the organization and gave them the opportunity to clean it up before naming them in public.

Piecework

Sometimes called 'job and finish', piecework is where the employee is paid per item. Most commonly used in industrial and production work, it is less popular now than in the past in traditional organizations because the volume of work possible is governed by production technology. It also

1   Home-working employees are provided with all the facilities and equipment that they would have if they were working on the employer's premises. For white collar staff this includes phone, computer, fax, stationery and access to copying, mail and postage facilities. For those engaged in production activities, this includes any tools of the trade, access to supplies and means of delivery. For those engaged in sales, this is likely to include a car as well as other office equipment.

2   Payment for home-working normally covers the use of any domestic equipment for work purposes (for example, telephone, computer, fax). It also normally includes paying an allowance in return for the member of staff using a part of their home as a workplace.

3   Home-workers feel isolated; this is often because they *are* isolated, cut off from the mainstream of their organization. Home-working requires the establishment of effective channels of communication. Regular face-to-face meetings, reviews of performance, the ability to discuss progress are essential and must form part of the way of working.

4   People must be prepared to cope with the lack of regular contact, the loss of social interaction, and regular attendance at a designated place of work.

5   Home-working must be fair to everyone concerned. Those who are not offered the chance of home-working feel let down. Those who are offered the chance of home-working often feel that they are being marginalized and that their opportunities for promotion and variation are limited.

tended to concentrate on volume rather than quality – and again, quality is now also governed by production technology to a greater extent.

This form of working is most common where people work on production activities at home and where they receive a fee per item completed. A form of piecework may also be used in administrative, clerical and secretarial activities where the payment is per 'batch' whereby an agreed fee is payable upon satisfactory completion of a batch or given volume of this work.

Honoraria and one-off payments

Honoraria and one-off payments are payable for work completed above and beyond normal duties. These are useful levers in promoting flexible working (provided they are not overused) in that they give the opportunity to employees to pursue project work and organizational interests (as well as their own) and create development and improvement that way.

Autonomous work groups and units

Autonomous work groups and units exist where there is a set amount of work to be carried out. How this is to be done is agreed between group members and their managers.

It is usual to work in line with organizational policies and aims. Performance is affected by technology, location and the nature of the relationship with the core organization.

Unit managers are responsible for getting the best out of the unit in the prevailing conditions. They are given resources and support from the centre: and this has to reconcile with autonomy and sufficient authority to act within these constraints.

The general attraction of this form of working is that it appears to address both the operational and psychological factors. Giving autonomy and deciding the allocation of work, organization of production, attention to quality and output based on broad performance targets (for example, 'to produce X amount of product Y to the given quality by deadline Z') leaves the group itself to arrange and determine how this is to be achieved. This means:

- full participation in determining and allocating the work, scheduling of priorities and activities, meeting preferences and gaining commitment to meeting the targets;
- responsibility in ensuring that the broad targets are met and that stages along the total schedule are also reached;
- esteem in that a complete output is seen at the end of activities with which the individual member of the group can identify;
- spirit and harmony in that the contribution of everyone involved can be seen and valued.

For autonomous working groups to be successful, high levels of skill and flexibility are required. Production technology and processes must be structured to meet behavioural as well as operational needs. Individual and group training and development is essential. The process is also greatly enhanced if the group is able to participate on the target-setting activities and to set its own means of quality control and assurance (see Summary Box 2.7).

Seasonal work

Seasonal work is used in order to cope with seasonal pressures (e.g. the production of items for Christmas; the production of ice cream and yoghurt for summer). From an organizational point of view, this means having the ability to call upon people with specific skills and attributes who are both capable and willing to work in this way. It also means paying sufficient attention to aspects of motivation, morale and identity if this form of working is to be optimized.

The Saab company's best-known experiment was at their engine factory at Sodertalje in Sweden. This began production in 1972. The company designed the factory layout of the work organization from scratch. The layout consisted of an oblong conveyor loop which moved engine blocks to seven assembly groups, each with three members. An island of potted plants enclosing a cafe with a telephone was placed alongside the assembly line. Each production group had its own U-shaped guide track in the floor to the side of the main conveyor loop. Engine blocks were taken from the main track, assembled by the group and then returned to the main track. They arrived with their cylinder heads already fitted and the group dealt with the final fitting of carburettors, distributors, spark plugs, cam shafts and other components. Each group assembled a completed engine and decided themselves how work was to be allocated. The guide track of each group was not mechanically driven. The group was simply given 30 minutes to complete each engine and they decided how that time would be spent.

Production faults were reduced by three-quarters. The company also made substantial savings on recruitment and training costs (because people were much more disposed to stay). Reductions were also clearly measurable in absenteeism and self-certificated sickness. The level of strikes, disputes and grievances also fell by three-quarters.

Networks

Networks are created in order to bring specific people and organizations together for specific activities. The great advantage to those creating the network is that organizational fixed costs and overheads are very low. This has, however, to be reconciled with the need to be able to create and maintain high levels of skill, quality and expertise when work is commissioned (see Summary Box 2.8).

On call

This is where individuals and groups do not work regularly for the organization, but where they may be called in at short notice to cover for sudden upturns in demand or to handle cases. Some on-call schemes pay a regular retainer; others include this in the form of increased payments when the work is actually carried out.

Subcontractors

Subcontractors are used to avoid extensive and expensive activities, functions, systems and procedures in which the organization has no particular expertise. Organizations pay fees to individuals and companies to carry out these activities. This form of activity is found extensively in the building and construction sectors. Many organizations now use it for catering,

SUMMARY BOX 2.8

Network creation: 'The Economist'

NI-CO was established in 1991 to sell the expertise and experience of the Northern Ireland public sector to overseas markets. It provides multi-disciplinary technical assistance packages, designed to meet the specific needs and requirements of its customers. NI-CO is currently delivering projects in several parts of Eastern Europe, the former Soviet Union, Africa and Central-South America.

The company has experienced substantial growth and now wishes to make further key appointments to its dynamic business team.

Public Administration Reform Specialists

To meet continued increase in demand for our services in this sector, NI-CO are urgently seeking long and short-term experts for work primarily, but not exclusively, in Eastern Europe and former Soviet Union.

C.V.s are sought from public service specialists with experience of:
- Organisation, Functional and Structural Reviews.
- Implementation of Efficiency Evaluation Exercises.
- Institutional Strengthening Measures.
- Human Resource Development Strategies.
- Development and Delivery of Vocational Training Measures.
- Civil Service Legislation and Procedures.
- Policy Development Measures.
- Political/Administrative Interfaces at central, regional and municipal levels.

Proven experience with the main international funding agencies is expected. Language skills, while preferred, are not essential.

International Consultancy and Procurement Services

We are currently expanding our data-base of panel consultants. If you have a proven track record gained through working on Bilateral or Multilateral Donor Funded Programmes world-wide and would like to be included on our data-base, please send your CV, along with any other relevant information to the address given below.

We are particularly interested in consultants with experience in the sectors detailed below but consultants from other sectors are also encouraged to register with us:

- International Procurement
- Transport and Logistics
- Privatisation and Restructuring
- Organisational Development and Training
- SME Development

- Educational Services
- Health
- Institutional Strengthening
- Agriculture
- Financial Services

In addition, we are very interested to hear from technical equipment experts with developing country experience, based in London and the South East who would be interested in joining our panel of experts to provide short term assistance to our Procurement Department in preparation of technical specifications and supply tender evaluations.

security, cleaning and car leasing services. The subcontracting approach is bounded only by the imagination of organizations. It is possible to sub-contract personnel and financial services, purchasing and supply, transport and distribution. In some sectors (e.g. telecommunications) much more mainstream and specialized work is also contracted out to satellite, subsidiary or 'networked' organizations.

Agencies and specialists

Agencies and specialists are used to enhance particular aspects of organization performance. They are not a substitute for regular in-house expertise.

- Staff and employment agencies are used to fill short-term gaps (e.g. sickness cover). Agency staff should never constitute the regular workforce.
- Executive search and head-hunters are used where they have special-ist knowledge of particular fields and are certain to produce a better result (quality of candidate, quality of short list) than if the organiza-tion were to do the work themselves.
- Marketing agencies and consultants are used as a fresh pool of ideas and to speed up the design and implementation of marketing cam-paigns. They are also a good source of consumer research statistics, buying and selling patterns.
- Software agencies and consultants are used to supply off-the-shelf packages or to design or refine these for particular applications. Relationships with software agencies also normally include training in the packages which have been bought.
- Production and production systems design agencies and consultants are used where the organization has a clear idea of what it needs to do but is less certain about how best to do it.
- Problem-solving agencies are used for handling crises such as arbitra-tion in disputes, handling industrial tribunal cases, rectifying serious breakdowns, serious public relations problems, putting right emer-gencies and crises. They are normally extremely expensive; but in return for this, they undertake to put the matter right or mitigate the damage quickly and effectively.

NOTES

1   For all activities carried out by outsiders, some form of *service level arrangement* is essential. This is to ensure that both parties know where they stand at the outset and the basis on which satisfaction is achieved and fees are paid. This is either a *service level contract,* in which every-thing is itemized and specified; or a *service level agreement,* in which a broader remit is given and received and which again states or strongly indicates the acceptable level of performance (see Summary Box 2.9).

SUMMARY BOX 2.9

Service level arrangements, agreements and contracts: content

Whether the service level is defined by agreement, arrangement or contract the following are essential:

- Agreement on the quality and volume of work to be carried out.
- Agreement on method and intervals of payment.
- Agreement on quality assurance procedures.
- The establishment of a form of liaison, consultation and communication.
- Establishment of a forum for solving problems, crises and emergencies.
- The ability to bring all parties together (or their representatives) when work factors or other issues demand.
- A means of arbitration or dispute reconciliation when it cannot be solved any other way.
- Establishment of the means by which the agreement, arrangement or contract is to be extended or terminated.
- Establishment of specific objects and targets so that accurate assessment of success or failure of the agreement arrangement or contract is easily established.

2   When using outsiders it is usual to pay a proportion of the fee at the point of initial agreement. A further proportion is payable on completion of the work. The final instalment is normally delayed until between 3–6 months after completion. This is to ensure that what was undertaken really works. This fee structure may be divided into equal parts, though increasingly organizations are adopting a 25-25-50 approach, with half the fee kept back in order to prove that what was proposed really works (see Summary Box 2.10).

3   Problems with subcontractors and agencies arise most often when there are misunderstandings over the volume and quality of work required.

4   If fee levels are too low, good subcontractors will be driven out of the area. Poor contractors only will be available.

5   Subcontracting incurs the attention of the Inland Revenue. Regular subcontracting, especially by individuals, is increasingly likely to be deemed to constitute employee status and organizations may be ordered to put these people on their payroll – whatever the actual nature or pattern of work.

6   Whatever the form or structure of work, quality has to be assured. This means reference to the quality of the working environment (whatever that is), quality of the supervisory/managerial arrangement (again, whatever that is) and also the quality of the product or service in hand. The critical step is therefore to understand that these factors have to be addressed and that suitable systems and procedures have to be put in hand and operated to ensure that this takes place (see Summary Box 2.11).

The following table illustrates some examples of fee-paying arrangements:

Example	Initial payment	Interim payment	Final payment
Architecture and design	Nominal	Upon initial agreement/contract	Upon delivery of the agreed design
Employment agency	Nominal	Upon satisfactory engagement	Upon completion of a specified term
Head hunters	25%	25%	50% upon completion of an agreed period
Retainers	Nominal	Upon engagement (sometimes in form of down-payment)	Upon completion of contract
Software agency	25%	25%	50%
Home-based work	Nil	Nil	100%
Expert services	Nil/nominal	By arrangement	Balance

SUMMARY BOX 2.10

Fee-paying arrangements

At this stage, it is useful to identify, from an organization and individual point of view, the factors and features required in any working relationship. These apply in all circumstances, whichever of the patterns indicated above are adopted.

Organization	Individual
Productive effort	Comfort
Effective workforce	Warmth
Effective individuals	Belonging
Effective groups	Contact
Continuous development	Success
New talents and energies	Fulfilment
Work harmony	Esteem
Expectations	Achievement
Job proficiency	Professionalism
Professionalism	Expectations and rewards
Success and value	Training, development and improvement

The two lists represent different sides of the same coin. Flexible work patterns have therefore to be designed and devised to bring them together, to match up and harmonize the pressures. Some of these pressures are convergent, others divergent; all have to be integrated and interrelated. Where this is not possible, potential areas and problems should at least be recognized.

SUMMARY BOX 2.11

The basis of a flexible environment

CONCLUSIONS   Organizations and their managers must ensure that, whoever is employed on whatever basis, they receive the same basic treatment. Part-time working has traditionally been viewed as a low-status, secondary form of employment. This is a negative and divisive attitude.

The hours worked by individuals should be long enough to produce effective work, regular enough to build successful working relationships, and flexible enough to accommodate personal preferences and commitments.

Structuring and maintaining effective flexible work requires planning and consideration at the outset because this is to form the basis of the organization's structure, and product and service delivery. Proper planning also ensures that any changes are much more easily accommodated than constantly working hand-to-mouth.

When outsiders and subcontractors are used they should conform to required organization norms, patterns of behaviour and conduct.

The whole purpose is to give the organization strength in dealing with its customers and carrying out its activities. Staff and expertise can be drawn from a wide range of backgrounds, bringing with them talents, qualities and capabilities that would not otherwise be available.

The main lesson lies in understanding the opportunities and constraints of different patterns of work and who these can be harnessed and applied to in particular situations.

Chapter 3

Contractual arrangements

A contract of employment exists once an offer of work has been made and accepted. This is normally confirmed in writing. All employees are bound by contracts of employment, whatever their length of service or hours worked. A contract of employment consists of the following:

CONTRACTS OF EMPLOYMENT

- stated terms;
- implied terms;
- attention to specific aspects of employment law;
- employer obligations;
- employee obligations.

Stated terms

Stated terms of employment consist of:

1. The letter of offer of employment which must state:

- the name and address of the employer;
- the name of the employee;
- where work is to be carried out;
- the title of the job;
- an indication of the work to be carried out;
- the hours to be worked;
- rates and methods of pay;
- other benefits (e.g. entitlements to paid holidays, membership of BUPA, use of company car and other equipment);
- any specific obligations (e.g. uniform, other dress code, requirements to be trained and developed).

2. Organizational procedures and practices:

- staff handbooks;
- collective agreements;
- discipline, grievance and dismissal arrangements;
- health and safety and emergency procedures.

3. Other written information:

- the content of the job advertisement;
- organizational particulars and information;
- any other organization papers which indicate particular ways of working standards, expectations and impressions.

4. Any information given orally:

- at interview;
- in other general discussions;
- in any other way, at any other time.

Implied terms

- Implications of the job title and description. For example, there is a common understanding of the duties of a secretary, a supervisor, a manager, a cashier, a cleaner, as well as distinctive organizational requirements. How the work is to be carried out is reinforced at the induction stage.
- Required attitudes and approaches (which are normally made clear at induction).
- Customer practice, indicating the reality of the working environment.

Obligations

- *Employer:* to provide adequate equipment for the work to be carried out effectively; to provide workplace insurance; to provide suitable training and development; to set and maintain standards of care, behaviour and attitudes; to indicate modes of address; to treat everybody equally and fairly; to provide a healthy and safe working environment; to take absolute care of employees; to provide specific provision for emergencies; to indicate specific hazardous and dangerous areas of activity.
- *Employee:* to work to the best of capabilities; to carry out stated and implied duties as directed or requested; to act in a safe and responsible manner at all times; to act in the employer's best interests.

Expectations

- *Employer:* employers are entitled to expect that if someone has applied for a job, they are basically capable and qualified to do it. They are entitled to end the contract if it becomes clear that the employee is not capable.
- *Employee:* the employee is entitled to expect that the work to be done is as stated or implied in the job advertisement, job description and other information. They are entitled to sue for breach of contract if it becomes clear that this is not the case.

Flexible contracts

The contractual form used is as described above. Particulars of flexible arrangements – hours, location, nature of work – are written in as appropriate, together with details of any additional obligations or requirements (e.g. expenses for travelling to different locations; different payment rates applying to various duties).

Flexibility of work and/or hours is made clear at the outset, stated in the contract, so that everyone knows where they stand. If there is the certainty, likelihood or possibility that work, location or hours may change, this also is made clear at the outset.

Ideally the contract is presented to new employees at the commencement of employment. They should be taken through it point by point. Any problems or difficulties are resolved at the outset. It is then signed by the new employee and an employer's representative. Again, everyone is then clear where they stand.

The contract should be of a standard format held on disk. Individual particulars can then be inserted. Enough space is left on the standard format to enable:

- hours;
- duties;
- locations;
- any other certain, likely or possible variations;

to be inserted according to the particular agreement. In this way, bureaucracy and administration are kept to a minimum. The whole can then be transferred to the file of the new employee.

Varying the contract

Contracts may be changed or varied at any time as the result of operational necessity. The purpose is to come to an arrangement that is satisfactory, both to employer and employee.

The minimum period of consultation for this purpose required by law is four weeks. This is greatly extended if a major rearrangement is required – such as relocation, a significant change of occupation, working days or hours.

Employers are required to act fairly and reasonably in all cases. Where flexible contracts and flexible working are clearly the norm, there is a much greater latitude and freedom to manoeuvre than where these are rigid.

As long as adequate and suitable assistance and training are provided, consultation is carried out, and operational necessity is demonstrated, employees are required to accede to any variations.

Terminating the contract

Other than employee resignation, the usual reasons for termination are:

- persistent breaches of discipline;
- gross misconduct (instances and examples of gross misconduct should always be indicated);
- lack of capability to do the job;
- where work has ceased or diminished (i.e. redundancy);

- some other substantial reason (such as incurring a jail sentence or serious illness which makes it impossible to continue to work).

Under flexible working, the main consideration is redundancy. It is both expensive and demoralizing to all staff when redundancies occur. The purpose of engaging the flexible approach is to have a fully capable multi-skilled and positive workforce. The attitude must be that redundancy is only to be used as a last resort. If people have shown themselves willing and able to be retrained, redeployed and moved around in the past, this is a much better alternative when one form of work ceases or diminishes.

There are legal requirements to consult on redundancies as soon as possible, with specific periods according to the numbers affected.

Equality of treatment

By law, as well as a matter of common sense, everyone is entitled to basic equality of treatment, regardless of length of service or hours worked (see Summary Box 3.1).

Basic standards of attitude and behaviour should apply to all. First-name terms should ideally apply across the entire organization as the formality of surname or job title terms is in itself a barrier to full flexibility. It also smacks of tradition – the way things were done; rather than flexibility – the way things should now be done.

Basic terms and conditions should apply to all. If one person has to clock or sign in, this should apply to all. There should be one staff handbook, one set of rules and procedures and these are to apply to everyone. Apart from anything else, this greatly reduces the administrative and bureaucratic burden.

Any view that is taken that some jobs, functions, departments or divisions are 'more important' necessarily means that others are 'less important'. It is a negative attitude, directly and immediately affecting those in the 'less important' areas. It also affects those in the 'more important' areas, who take steps and use resources to protect and enhance their position rather than in the pursuit of profitable and effective activities.

This does not mean equality of salary. Differentials are clearly made on the basis of expertise, responsibility, authority and hours worked. Differentials should never be made on any other basis. Discrimination on grounds of victimization, harassment, bullying should normally at least be a disciplinary offence, and many organizations list this under gross misconduct. Discrimination on grounds of race, ethnic origin, sex/ gender, religion, marital status, membership/refusal to join a trade union, and spent convictions (with many exceptions) is illegal.

Opportunities for variety, training and development, project work and secondments are made available to everyone based on capability and potential, regardless of length of service or hours worked. Under flexible

There are three boundaries to equality at the workplace – legislation, best practice and organizational attitudes.

Legislation

It is illegal in the UK to discriminate between employees on grounds of: gender; race and ethnic background; disability; membership of a trade union or refusal to join a trade union; convictions for offences committed in the past which are deemed to be 'spent'.

The only exceptions normally available are where there is 'a genuine occupational qualification' – where for matters of normal common decency or overwhelming social expectation an employee of a specific gender or racial/ethnic background may be appointed in preference to others.

Best practice

'Best practice' has no legal force – it is rather a combination of the highest level of general understanding of human resource/personnel behaviour and practice, combined with guidelines issued by specific professional bodies (e.g. ACAS, The Institute of Personnel and Development) which state that quite apart from anything else, unreasonable discrimination on any of the following grounds is likely to edit out great swathes of the work-force from which useful, effective, capable and willing staff may be drawn.

The areas covered by best practice are: age; location (some organizations refuse to take staff from a given place); school/college/university background; medical history – unless there is a direct relationship between a current or previous medical condition and the work to be carried out; size, height and appearance; previous employment history – again, unless anything in it directly militates against their likely effectiveness as a current employee.

Attitude

Underpinning all aspects of 'equality' are attitudes of fairness and reasonableness, and ordinary common decency and humanity. These attitudes are apparent at four levels – corporate, managerial, group and individual. It is essential that they all accord with the principles of fairness and decency. It is also essential that any misdemeanour, discrimination, victimization, bullying or harassment is treated as a very serious offence and dealt with directly whenever it becomes apparent.

working, this is arranged through a combination of organization demand; personal preference and interest; and professional, technical and occupational expertise.

Differentials in relative status and value are avoided if everyone is treated in this way and put on the same basic terms and conditions and standards of attitude and behaviour.

Fixed-term contracts

Fixed-term contracts are the same as normal contracts of employment, except that the date on which the contract is to end is stated. Fixed-term contracts may be of any duration suitable to the organization – for example some local government bodies and health authorities place their senior managers on fixed-term contracts of up to seven years. The date of termination is stated at the outset of employment and is normally:

- a specified date in the future;
- an indicated date – for example, in a fixed-term contract covering maternity leave, it is permissible to use the phrase 'when employee X returns from maternity leave';
- where the contract is for the duration of a project, it is usual to use the phrase 'when the project ends'.

NOTES

1   For any contract that lasts more than two years a redundancy or severance payment is normally required at the end. Employees can be persuaded to waive their rights to this, but it is usual to make some form of payment in return for this. In any case, employees must know what they are doing, and why, and must not be coerced or cajoled down this route. Failure to do this normally constitutes breach of contract.

2   For any fixed-term contract that is renewed so that the total period of continuous employment is more than two years, a redundancy or severance payment is usually required as above.

3   If an employee breaks a fixed-term contract (i.e. leaves before it ends), it is open for the employer to sue him/her for breach of contract. However, this rarely occurs in practice because of the time, expense, inconvenience and (invariably) adverse publicity involved.

4   If an employee on a fixed-term contract is clearly not up to the standard required it is possible to cancel the contract on the grounds that the employee has breached it because of their lack of capability. The onus is placed entirely on the employer to prove this. If standards and capabilities are not clearly specified the employee is placed in a strong position to defend the cancellation. Where the case goes against the employer, courts normally make an award to the employee of the equivalent of the rest of their entitlement under the terms of the contract.

5   Where it becomes essential to extend the fixed-term contract – for example, where a project is not completed to time or where maternity leave has been extended for some reason – it is quite legitimate to do this on a week-by-week or month-by-month basis. However, once again, any extension that takes the period of continuous employment over two years normally incurs obligations to pay redundancy or severance at the end.

6   For fixed-term contracts, it is both useful and legitimate to make some form of bonus or additional final payment at the end of the contract. This is only payable upon satisfactory completion by the employee. The final payment can either take the form of:

- *an additional payment.* This means that effectively the employee is being overpaid. The trade-off for this is the fact that the employee is no longer retained on the payroll and has no longer to be accommodated or provided with equipment and services. The additional payment may therefore be seen as a relatively small price to pay; or
- *money withheld over the period of the contract pending its satisfactory completion.* Withholding may be overt or covert. The overt is where both parties have agreed to this beforehand. The covert is where the withholding is presented to the employee as a bonus, but where what has really happened is that the employer has offered the employee the contract based on a less irregular wage or salary, and that only by achieving the bonus do they make 100% of what the employer is prepared to pay.

Any form of final payment should be stated and understood at the commencement of employment.

Subcontracting

Contracts for subcontractors do not constitute a contract of employment. They concentrate entirely on the level, volume and quality of product or service required. It is usual to specify at the outset of the contract:

- the fee structure;
- the volume of work;
- the quality required;
- the duration of the contract;
- how performance and satisfaction are to be assessed;
- any other material, stated or implied issues.

How the work is carried out is a matter for the subcontractor. It is both necessary and quite legitimate for regular progress meetings to be convened. It is also essential to have general and continuing effective liaison and communication. Within standards of attitude, behaviour and performance specified, and which are the norms at the contracting organization, subcontracted work is carried out by the subcontractor in ways which they see fit.

NOTES

1   Contract timescales have to be sufficiently long to give the relationship a chance to work effectively; this has to be balanced against the threat of being tied in to an expensive and unproductive relationship.

2 Where there is a change from employee to self-employed status, the ex-employee becomes responsible for their tax, national insurance and the keeping of accounts. The ex-employee is also likely to have to provide their own equipment in the future. There is no security of tenure and no obligation (on either part) for any contract to be reviewed once completed. There is at least a moral responsibility on the employer to make all of this clear.

3 All subcontracting arrangements may legitimately be varied by agreement between the two parties.

4 Subcontractors may not be prevented from carrying out activities elsewhere provided that these do not interfere with the particular contract. The only exception to this is where commercial confidentiality or a conflict of interest is considered to be present; and the onus is entirely on the contracting organization to prove this.

EMPLOYMENT LAW

All employees are entitled to employment protection after two years' continuous service whatever the hours worked. Anyone – whether designated full-time or part-time – may claim unfair dismissal if they lose their job for no good or demonstrable reason after two years' continuous service.

All employees are entitled not to be victimized or discriminated against on grounds of race, gender, disability, membership of a trade union, refusal to join a trade union or a spent conviction for a criminal offence, regardless of length of service or hours worked.

All female employees are entitled to 14 weeks' maternity leave if they become pregnant, regardless of length of service or hours worked. All female employees of more than two years' continuous service are entitled to 29 weeks maternity leave, regardless of hours worked. All pregnant employees are entitled to return to their old job or one not substantially different and on the same pay, terms and conditions of employment as when they left. If the pay has risen in the meantime, they are entitled to the new rate.

All employees are entitled to one week's notice after four weeks' continuous employment regardless of hours worked. If the contract specifies more than this, then the higher amount must be given.

All employees are entitled to fair treatment in cases of discipline, grievance and dismissal, regardless of length of service or hours worked. They must be given the opportunity to hear the case against them and state their point of view. They are entitled to representation at each stage. They are entitled to receive confirmation in writing of the decision and to appeal against this if they so wish.

The distinction between full- and part-time employment is becoming **CONCLUSIONS** ever more blurred. There is now no set number of hours which is deemed to constitute a full-time job. 1995 guidelines issued by the Department for Employment and the Advisory, Conciliation and Arbitration Service (ACAS) recommend that all employees are treated exactly the same regardless of length of service or hours worked. This is normally the benchmark for questions that arise over 'fairness and reasonableness of treatment' and 'best practice'.

It is also clear that many hitherto part-time, broken or intermittent contracts are now regarded in law as continuous employment. This is now more or less certain where agreed periods of paid leave are taken – for example, with term time and other 'hours around children' employment patterns. Employers which allow their employees periods of extended leave, sabbaticals and career breaks must acknowledge the period of continuous service when the employee returns to work.

It is likely that the period of exclusion from employment protection will be reduced from two years to one year in the near future. If and when this occurs, it is certain to apply to all employees, whatever their hours of work or pattern of employment.

Chapter 4

Motivation and rewards

Motivation is a reflection of the reasons why people do things. All behaviour has purposes. All behaviour is therefore based on choice: people choose to do the things they do. Sometimes this choice is very restricted (sink or swim for example). Sometimes it is constrained by the law (for example, stopping the car when the traffic lights are red). And again, it is constrained by the norms and processes of society: for example, people tend to wear smart clothes to a party where they know that everybody else will be well dressed. In each case however, there is a choice, though the propensity, encouragement and direction to choose one course of action rather than another in the examples given is strong, if not overwhelming.

The ability to gain the commitment and motivation of staff in organizations has been recognized as important in certain sectors of the business sphere. It is now more universally accepted as a critical business and organizational activity, and one that has highly profitable returns and implications for the extent of the returns on investment made in the human resource.

There is a direct correlation between going to a lot of trouble to motivate staff and profitable business performance. In the first place, the ability to motivate staff in the workplace stems from understanding the following:

1 A general appreciation of how human beings *behave* in particular situations, and in response to their needs to satisfy and fulfil basic drives, instincts, needs and wants. Some of these are instinctive, others are the product of the civilization in which they live, and the socialization processes contained therein. Others still are the product of the occupation held by the individual and the education, training, ethics, standards and aspirations thus instilled. Finally, the organization itself impinges on the behaviour of the human being, in terms of the structure, style, shared values and work practices adopted.

2 An understanding of the nature of the *work* that must be carried out, and the effects that this will have, or is likely to have, on those who are to do it. This has to do with the extent of intrinsic satisfaction and fulfilment that is present in the work; the interface between the human resource and technology; and, again the style of management and supervision that is to be adopted.

3   The wider standards and expectations of the *relationships* between humans at the workplace. The background and aura for this is created by management, and infuses everyone (positively or negatively) at the workplace. At its best, it contains a variety of elements including: enthusiasm and commitment on the part of everyone to the organization and its products, services and customers; a corporate belief in the organization and all its works: a measure of involvement in the implementation of policy and achievement of objectives by all concerned; a clearly established and understood set of principles and operational standards by which the organization functions: the taking of pride by all members of staff in the organization and all its works; adequate, effective and relevant communication processes and methods: and preventative approaches to problems and commitment to resolve them quickly when they arise.

Conversely, there must be a recognition, on the part of organizations and their managers, that where these elements are not present, or where they are diluted, not believed in, or not valued, there will be a tendency towards de-motivation and alienation on the part of the staff.

4   Organizations *cannot be all things to all people.* They can only accommodate a range of divergent interests and aspirations among the staff insofar as these can be made to accord with their overall purposes and values. Dysfunctions arising from their divergences and conflicts of interest are most common in multinational hierarchies, and public and health services, where the organization style and structure is either inefficient, or irrelevant, to the true purpose of the organization concerned.

The major theories of motivation are as follows.

MOTIVATION THEORIES

Rensis Likert: System 4

Likert's contribution to the theories of workplace motivation arose from his work with high-performing managers; managers and supervisors who achieved high levels of productivity, low levels of cost and high levels of employee motivation, participation and involvement at their places of work. The work demonstrated a correlation between this success and the style and structure of the work groups that they created. The groups achieved not only high levels of economic output and therefore wage and salary targets, but were also heavily involved both in group maintenance activities and the design and definition of work patterns. This was underpinned by a supportive style of supervision and the generation of a sense of personal worth, importance and esteem in belonging to the group itself.

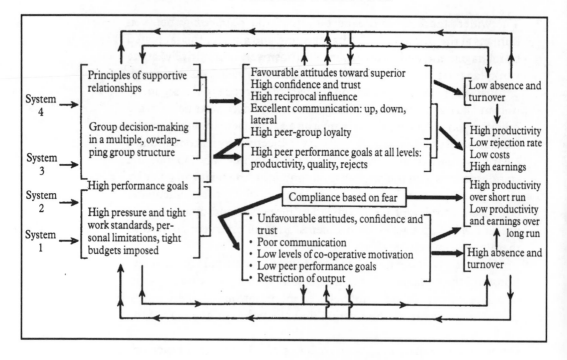

Figure 4.1

To demonstrate the interrelationship and interaction of the variables defined, and present a spectrum of organization and management performance levels.

(Source: Likert, 1961)

The System 4 model arose from this work. Likert identified four styles or systems of management:

- *System 1: Exploitative Authoritative,* where power and direction come from the top downwards and where there is no participation, consultation or involvement on the part of the workforce. Workforce compliance is thus based on fear. Unfavourable attitudes are generated, there is little confidence and trust, and low levels of motivation to co-operate or generate output above the absolute minimum.

- *System 2: Benevolent Authoritative,* which is similar to System 1 but which allows some 'upward' opportunity for consultation and participation in some areas. Again attitudes tend to be generally unfavourable; confidence, trust and communication are also at low levels. In both Systems 1 and 2, productivity may be high over the short run when targets can be achieved by a combination of coercion and bonus and overtime payments. However, both productivity and earnings are demonstrably low over the long run; there is also high absenteeism and labour turnover.

- *System 3: Consultative,* where aims and objectives are set after discussion and consultation with subordinates; where communication is two-way and where teamwork is encouraged at least in some areas. Attitudes towards both superiors and the organization tend to be favourable especially when the organization is working steadily. Productivity tends to be higher, absenteeism and turnover lower. There is also demonstrable reduction in scrap, improvement in product quality, reduction in overall operational costs and higher levels of earning on the part of the workforce.

- *System 4: Participative,* in which three basic concepts have a very important effect on performance – the use by the manager of the principle of supportive relationships throughout the work group; the use of group decision-making and group methods of supervision; and the setting of high performance and very ambitious goals for the department and also for the organization overall. This was Likert's preferred System.

Abraham Maslow: a hierarchy of needs

The hierarchy of needs is normally depicted as a pyramid. The hierarchy of needs works from the bottom of the pyramid upwards. It shows the most basic needs and motivations at the lowest levels while those at the top are created by, or fostered by, civilization and society.

Maslow identified five key needs:

1 *Physiological:* the need for food, drink, air, warmth, sleep and shelter; basic survival needs related to the instinct for self-preservation.
2 *Safety and security:* protection from danger, threats or deprivation and the need for stability (or relative stability) of environment.
3 *Social:* a sense of belonging to a society and its groups; for example: the family, the organization, the work group; the giving and receiving of friendship; basic status needs within these groups, and the need to participate in social activities.
4 *Esteem needs:* self-respect, self-esteem, appreciation, value, recognition and status both on the part of the individuals concerned and the society, circle or group in which they interrelate: part of the esteem

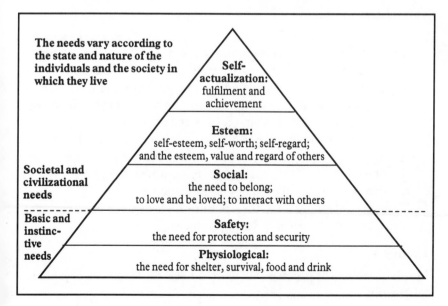

Figure 4.2

A hierarchy of needs

(Source: Maslow, 1987)

need is therefore the drive to gain the respect, esteem and appreciation accorded by others.

5   *Self-actualization:* the need for self-fulfilment, self-realization, personal development, accomplishment, mental, material and social growth and the development and fulfilment of the creative faculties.

This was the hierarchy of needs outlined. Maslow reinforced his model by stating that people tended to satisfy their needs systematically. They started with the basic, instinctive needs and then moved up the hierarchy. Until one particular group of needs was satisfied, a person's behaviour would be dominated by them. Thus the hungry or homeless person will look to their needs for self-esteem and society only after their hunger has been satisfied and they have found a place to stay. The other point that Maslow made was that people's motives were constantly being modified as their situation changed, and in relation to their levels of adaptation and other perceptual factors. This was especially true of the self-actualization needs in which having achieved measures of fulfilment and recognition, man nevertheless tended to remain unsatisfied and to wish to progress further.

Douglas McGregor: Theory X and Theory Y

McGregor identified two distinctive sets of assumptions made by managers about employees. From this he articulated two extreme attitudes or views and called them Theory X and Theory Y. His thesis was that in practice most people would come somewhere between the two, except in certain circumstances.

Theory X

This is based on three premises:

1   People *dislike work* and will avoid it if they can. They would rather be directed than accept any responsibility; indeed, they will avoid authority and responsibility if they possibly can. They have no creativity except when it comes to getting around the rules and procedures of the organization; above all they will not use their creativity in the pursuit, either of the job or the interests of the organization.

2   They must be *forced or bribed* to put out the right effort. They are motivated mainly by money which remains the overriding reason why they go to work. Their main anxiety concerns their own personal security, which they alleviate by earning money.

3   They are *inherently lazy,* they require high degrees of supervision, coercion and control in order to produce adequate output.

Theory Y

This is based on the premise that work is necessary to man's psychological growth:

1 People *wished only to be interested in their work,* and under the right conditions they will enjoy it. They gain intrinsic fulfilment from it; they are motivated by the desire to realize their own potential, to work to the best of their capabilities and to employ the creativity and ingenuity with which they are endowed in the pursuit of this.

2 They will *direct themselves* towards given, accepted and understood targets; they will seek and accept responsibility and authority; and they will accept the discipline of the organization in the pursuit of this. They also impose their own self-discipline on themselves and their activities.

Whatever the conditions, management was to be responsible for organizing the elements of productive enterprise and its resources in the interests of economic ends. This would be done in ways suitable to the nature of the organization and its workforce in question; either providing a coercive style of management and supervision or arranging a productive and harmonious environment in which the workforce can and will take responsibility for erecting their own efforts and those of their unit towards organizational aims and objectives.

Frederick Herzberg: Two Factor Theory

The research of Herzberg was directed at people in places of work. It was based on questioning people in organizations in different jobs, at different levels, to establish:

1 those factors that led to *extreme dissatisfaction* with the job, the environment and the workplace; and

2 those factors that led to *extreme satisfaction* with the job, the environment and the workplace.

The factors giving rise to satisfaction Herzberg called *motivators.* Those giving rise to dissatisfaction he called *hygiene factors.*

The motivators that emerged were: achievement, recognition, the nature of the work itself, level of responsibility, advancement, and opportunities for personal growth and development. These factors are all related to the actual content of the work and job responsibilities. These factors, where present in a working situation, led to high levels and degrees of satisfaction on the part of the workforce.

The hygiene factors or dissatisfiers identified were: company policy and administration; supervision and management style; levels of pay and salary; relationships with peers; relationships with subordinates; status; and security. These are factors that, where they were good or adequate, would not in themselves make people satisfied; by ensuring that they were indeed adequate, dissatisfaction was removed but satisfaction was not in itself generated. On the other hand, where these aspects were bad, extreme dissatisfaction was experienced by all respondents.

Figure 4.3

Two-factor or
hygiene factor
theory

(Source:
Herzberg, 1974)

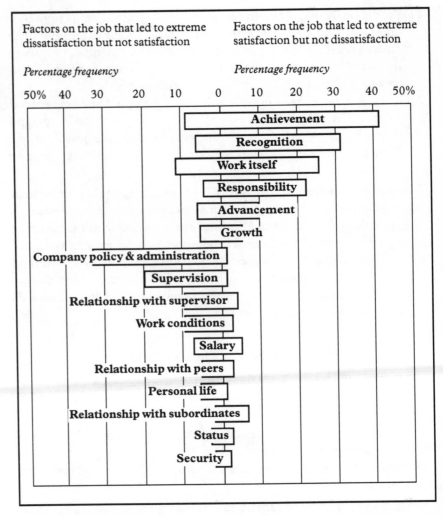

Organizations that failed to provide adequate hygiene factors tended to have high levels of conflict, absenteeism and labour turnover, and low general morale.

Expectancy

The expectancy approach to motivation draws a relationship between:

- the expectations that people have in work situations;
- the efforts that they put in to meet these expectations;
- the rewards offered for successful efforts.

Understanding individual aspirations and the extent to which work can satisfy these is essential. It is also necessary to recognize the need to balance expectation, effort and reward. If expectations are raised and then not fulfilled, effort declines. If high levels of effort turn out to be unproductive, expectations are re-positioned downwards. If the anticipated rewards are not forthcoming, effort declines. The effect of each is always to demotivate and demoralize.

This is clearly centred on the individual. It relates to the ways in which the individual sees or perceives the environment. In particular, it relates to his view of work, his expectations, aspirations, ambitions and desired outcomes from it, and the extent to which these can be satisfied at the workplace or carrying out the occupation in question. For example, the individual may have no particular regard for the job that they are currently doing but will nevertheless work productively and effectively at it and be committed to it because it is a stepping stone in their view to greater things – and these are the expectations that they have of it and constitutes the basis of their efforts and the quality of these efforts. This is compounded however by other factors – the actual capacities and aptitudes of the individual concerned on the one hand and the nature of the work environment on the other. It is also limited by the perceptions and expectations that the commissioner of the work has on the part of the person who is actually carrying it out. There is a distinction to be drawn between the effort put into performance and the effectiveness of that effort – hard work, conscientiously carried out, does not always produce effective activity; the effort has to be directed and targeted. There has also to be a match between the rewards expected and those that are offered – a reward is merely a value judgement placed on something offered in return for effort, and if this is not valued by the receiver it has no effect on his motivation.

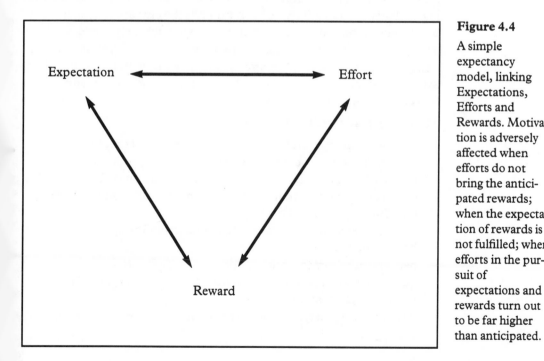

Figure 4.4

A simple expectancy model, linking Expectations, Efforts and Rewards. Motivation is adversely affected when efforts do not bring the anticipated rewards; when the expectation of rewards is not fulfilled; when efforts in the pursuit of expectations and rewards turn out to be far higher than anticipated.

WORK MOTIVATION

There are a number of common threads that run through each of the theories. Motivation is above all a 'joint venture' – organizations are entitled to expect motivation on the part of the people who come to work for them; and in turn, they must ensure that motivation is provided for the people who come to work for them

High levels of work motivation are based on:

- demanding, interesting, varied and valuable work that people are capable of carrying out; recognizing and rewarding their achievements; taking early remedial action when standards fall;
- treating everyone equally and with respect; creating workplace relationships based on trust, honesty, openness and integrity;
- creating a unity of purpose and mutual interest between organization and staff;
- developing positive work, professional and personal relationships within and between groups;
- giving everyone the opportunity to progress and develop as far as they possibly can, whatever their occupation, salary level or personal aspirations;
- attending to individual needs, wants, drives, hopes, fears and aspirations; ensuring that everyone progresses, develops and improves operationally, professionally and personally;
- high, regular and increasing levels of pay in return for high quality work.

If all of this is in place, organizations are entitled to expect high quality, high value work. Creating these conditions is the organization's responsibility. The potential for this is much greater under flexible working arrangements because so many more of the conditions are easier to satisfy. Moreover, people are coming into flexible working with raised expectations of security, employability, variety and opportunity. The basis of the whole relationship is clear – and positive.

Motivation is adversely affected by:

- management style and the invisibility of managers and supervisors; inability to solve problems quickly; adversarial approaches to staff;
- physical and psychological distance, based again on visibility and also on forms of preferential treatment, inaccessibility and uncertainty (see Summary Box 4.1);
- bad interpersonal and inter-occupational relationships;
- boring and valueless work;
- bad and unclear communications, infrequently delivered and frequently changed; and where the message given does not relate to the reality of the situation;
- inherent dishonesty, lack of integrity and unfairness in the treatment of people.

Physical distance describes the proximity or otherwise of people to each other. It is affected by the physical environment – technology (where for example, work stations are determined by the design of the machinery); office and work premises layout; open and closed plan arrangements; the use of traditional production lines or autonomous work groupings; the dispersal of physical locations.

Psychological distance is the term used to describe the behavioural barriers that exist between individuals. These are reinforced or broken down by the presence or absence of: dress codes; status symbols; modes of address; organizational attitudes to different sectors of the workforce; differing terms and conditions of employment; different forms of staff representation and union recognition; feelings of isolation and alienation.

In flexible working, there is a strong propensity for both physical and psychological barriers to be present. Especially for those working away from the main work premises, or from home, or in the field, or in foreign countries these barriers potentially exist from a very early stage in the working relationship. It is essential that both their presence and their potential effects are recognized; and that management priorities, style and approach are designed to ensure that these are kept to a minimum.

It should also be noted that individual motivation changes as the relationship between people and their organization progresses. The motivations:

- to read the job advertisements;
- to apply for a job;
- to turn up for interview;
- to accept a job;
- to turn up on the first day;
- to turn up on the second day;
- to keep turning up;

are all different. The individual is affected by the ways in which they have been treated on each of these occasions and their motivation is either enhanced or diminished accordingly.

Under flexible working, motivation is most likely to be adversely affected by pay levels, the quality or the value of the work, matters of physical and psychological distance, and the form of supervision adopted.

Where pay is low, it is a mark of low esteem and value. It reflects the level of worth placed on the staff. The only exception to this is voluntary or vocational work; and vocation should never be confused with professionalism or expertise. It is both unfair and unethical to take advantage of people's commitment to their customers and clients.

Where work value is low, jobs, and therefore staff, are dispensable and those involved will know this better than anyone. Work of low value is extravagant and wasteful and is either to be abolished or improved.

Where product and service quality is low, there is no personal, professional or occupational feeling of satisfaction from being involved. Indeed, there is often a desire not to be associated. Real achievement is based on completing things that are good and positive and give satisfaction, not just on completing something. Especially with part-time or short hours working, this has to be produced very quickly.

People's motivation is directly affected by:

- *Expectations:* the outcomes that they anticipate as the result of being in a situation and carrying out work.
- *Efforts:* the amount of energy that they are prepared to put into the situation.
- *Rewards:* the benefits to be accrued by being in the particular situation.

Recognizing the balance between the three is vital. If rewards do not match expectations, efforts decline. If other expectations are not met, efforts decline. If rewards exceed expectations, efforts increase in the short term, though in the long term this becomes the new level of expectation.

Individuals – whatever their pattern of work or frequency of attendance – therefore act best when they have a reasonable expectation that their effort will lead to the desired rewards and outcomes. It also emphasizes the importance of the individual in any form of working relationship. It also indicates that raising expectations leads to the anticipation of enhanced rewards; and that lowering rewards reduces both expectations and effort.

Communication and understanding

Communication and understanding is the other main key to staff motivation. The nature, media, language, volume and quality of communications reinforces the working relationship. Again, where one or more of these elements is lacking or wrong, motivation suffers.

Communication is best and most effective face-to-face, supported in writing in clear, simple direct language. Communication always suffers when this is not present. It is also damaged when it is not supported by managerial or organizational actions or integrity. When this occurs, people always look for hidden meanings and messages. This is counterproductive to effective work, damaging and ultimately destroying working relationships.

Where face-to-face communication is not possible (e.g. for home-workers, sales staff and others working away from the organization for long periods), regular meetings are so convened to get over the problems caused by working in isolation. This is part of the investment and obligation entered into when creating a flexible workforce. These meetings should devote at least part of their time to general discussions about the overall state of affairs and filling in the outworkers on any and all matters of importance, general knowledge and concern. It is also the opportunity to ensure that achievements and successes are noted and recognized. Attendance at these meetings is compulsory. It is the only clear opportunity that organizations and their managers have of building on existing levels of confidence and identity, as well as resolving problems and points of contention. *Serious problems should always be tackled face-to-face. To attempt to tackle them by e-mail or over the telephone, or by fax, normally results in the situation getting worse.*

These conditions are present in all effective flexible working. Motivation of the flexible workforce is completed by:

- good and positive supervision which encourages and enhances rather than restricts;
- work satisfaction, based on flexible structuring, enrichment and variety;
- high levels of team, group and organizational identity;
- positive and professional relationships between group members and different groups and teams;
- recognition for work well done;
- recognizing communication problems that are likely to arise in specific situations and devising patterns of supervision and the means of communication that address these to best effect;
- an attitude that learns from failure rather than seeks to apportion blame;
- attention to the general working environment, adequate standards of accommodation and cleanliness, a standard of facilities with which people can be comfortable;
- relating status to work performance and organization membership rather than to job titles, group or department membership.

If all of this is in place, organizations are entitled to accept a reciprocal commitment from their employees, high levels of commitment and high standards and quality of work.

Fixed-term contracts

Problems often arise with fixed-term contracts when the staff member is coming to the end of the contract and there is no prospect of it being renewed. The main thrust is to ensure that the groundwork is done at the induction stage so that the individuals concerned know what is expected of them throughout the duration. This is supported by the 'final bonus' approach to pay (see page 33), where the money is only made up if the whole contract is completed satisfactorily. It is also supported by the style of supervision that (as with everything else) nips in the bud problems of attitude, behaviour or performance. From this point of view, fixed-term contract staff are no different to anyone else.

Those whose performance distinctly lapses in the last few months of the contract should be put through poor-performance procedures as quickly as possible. This either has the effect of raising performance or not. In the former case, well and good; in the latter, the organization has both grounds for terminating the contract forthwith and evidence to produce to defend any subsequent prosecution for breach of contract.

The ground rules are therefore clear at the outset. Fixed-term contract staff are treated exactly the same as anyone else. Opportunities afforded by the organization are open to fixed-term contract staff, the same as everyone else. The benefit lies in adopting a positive rather than a negative view.

If fixed-term contract staff are engaged for the duration of a project rather than a specified period of time, if they finish the project early it is often best to pay up the contract and let them go if there is nothing else that they can usefully be doing. A greater problem is likely to arise where a project overruns, and one of the duties of project managers (and those who manage project managers) is to ensure that the work is not being deliberately spun out.

Irregular work

Problems arise around the areas of identity, recognition and achievement. The best way to get over this is to make all part-time work as regular as possible. Where this is not possible, time needs to be found to integrate the irregular worker into the organization and with those with whom they have to work. It is often very difficult to build up a useful and positive working relationship when hours are too short or too infrequent; if this is the only approach possible in the circumstances, then the difficulty should be recognized and such steps as are possible in the circumstances taken.

NOTES

1   Some organizations compensate for dull, boring and unsatisfactory work by putting up wages, over-paying indeed. This only makes work more bearable, not more interesting. Indeed, it is counter-productive in some circumstances because people set themselves targets of gritting their teeth and working for a specific period of time to earn a set amount of money before quitting.

Dull, boring and unstretching work is also detrimental to both mental and physical health. Financial compensation therefore only addresses this problem in the short term. In the long term people may leave anyway; and the performance of those who do stay declines as their health is affected, whatever the level of pay. Where work is dull, boring and unsatisfactory, it should be restructured.

2   Best results from staff are achieved through increased levels and
requirements of commitment and achievement, use of talents and
qualities through the development and improvement of expertise,
work methods and the working environment. Not to do this, ultimately, has the standardizing and detrimental effect in all routine
aspects of work. Motivation and morale drop as does work interest –
and this applies to all types of work and levels of expertise.

High quality and flexible staff are well rewarded. This does not mean
overpaying. It does mean paying as much as is feasible in the circumstances. Pay should also be increased to reflect improvements in levels of
performance (especially organizational performance); expertise; and job
enlargement, especially where additional responsibility is taken on.

**PAY AND
BENEFITS**

Japanese companies, especially, working in the UK pay their staff
extremely well in return for full flexibility of working. The best paid car
workers in the UK work for Nissan, Toyota and Honda. The best paid elec-
tronics workers in the UK work for Sony, Sharp, Panasonic and Toshiba.
The view taken is that, in return for these high levels of pay and rewards, the
company is entitled to expect true quality and commitment to work.

Pay

The following elements of payment can be identified.

* *Payments:* annual, quarterly, monthly, four-weekly, weekly, daily,
  hourly; commission, bonus, increments, fees; profit, performance
  and merit-related payments.
* *Allowances:* attendance, disturbance, shift, weekend, unsocial hours,
  training and development, location and relocation, absence from
  home; special conditions – for example, dangerous and hazardous
  locations and occupations.

Payment mixes adopted by organizations in devising and implementing
reward strategies for different staff categories cover a variety of aims and
purposes in response to particular situations. The general purpose is to
address the following.

* *Expectations:* to meet the expectations of the job holder.
* *Attractiveness:* for the purposes of attracting and retaining staff.
* *Motivation:* based on value, effort, expertise and future commitment.
* *Mixes of payment with other aspects:* people in the UK expect to receive
  a 'reward package', a combination of pay with other benefits and
  rewards. This varies according to the particular situation.
* *Occupational aspects:* part of the reward package is likely to include the
  provision of specialist, expert and continuous training.

- *Performance and profit-related elements:* related either to the achievement of particular objectives, or to overall company performance.

    Where it is based on targets, the scheme must be believed in, valued and understood by all concerned. Targets must be achievable. They must be neither too easy nor too difficult. Targets must be set in advance; if they are achieved, payment must always be made. The purpose is to reward effort and achievement on the part of the staff.

Where pay is related to company profitability and performance, the best and fairest approach is to pay everyone the same percentage of their salary. For example, a 10% performance-related element would result in someone on £3,000 receiving a bonus of £300; for someone on £30,000, a bonus of £3,000 would be received; and so on (see Summary Box 4.2).

SUMMARY BOX 4.2

Semco

> Semco, the Brazilian industrial equipment manufacturer, takes a different view of this. The company works in autonomous business units.
>
> At the end of each quarter, the profit element accruing to each autonomous business unit is published to the staff who work in it and a profit-related pay element agreed. How the profit-related element is divided up among the staff is a matter for the staff concerned only – the company takes no part in prescribing how the money is to be divided up.
>
> Most of the business units take the profit-related elements and then divide it up equally among all those working. The result is to benefit those whose salaries are at the lower end of the scale. Whatever approach is chosen however, the company will support it.

Where performance is to be rewarded in the issuing of share options, this again should be on an equal basis. The availability of share options should be available to anyone who wants to take advantage of them: where restrictions are placed, again this should be done as a percentage of individual salary.

Where pay is related to team performance, all members should receive the same percentage bonus.

Where pay is related to individual performance, there must be absolute trust and confidence between assessor and assessee.

NOTES

1   If the hourly rate is too low, no effective wage/work relationship is possible. Pay is a mark of value, and low pay in the eyes of the employees means low value. People take low-paid jobs only because they have to and until something better comes along.

2   Turnover and absenteeism rise where the employees are, or perceive themselves to be, unvalued or undervalued. Productivity falls where employees are unvalued or undervalued.

3   Overpayment does not make mundane or boring work more interesting: it makes it more bearable (see motivation above). When pay rates rise, there is a short-term benefit. This is followed by employees reverting to previous levels of activity and approach.

4   Those who work from a variety of locations are normally provided with transport, travelling time and expenses and additional allowances. These are either paid separately or else worked into the total salary package.

5   Those who work on a variety of jobs, which change frequently or regularly, or whose hours and shift patterns change frequently and regularly, are provided with additional payments to compensate. This is done either by:

a) making a point of itemizing each of the elements included in the wage or salary. This satisfies the perceptions and expectations of employees. It requires additional administration and, in large organizations, with highly complex work hours and shift patterns, this is a heavy additional cost;

b) paying a relatively high single wage or salary in return for which the employee works as necessary and directed. This takes a greater level of introduction and understanding; the payback is to remove the administrative burden indicated above.

6   Integrity and equality. Any system of payment must be understood and valued. It should treat people equally and with respect.

There is never a sound or honest reason for rewarding one group of the workforce at the expense of others. The effect is always to demoralize those who lose out. The longer-term effect is to enhance any divisions that already exist between the different elements of the workforce as they jockey for position to ensure that they are not the ones to lose out in the future.

7   By law, an itemized pay statement is required for all employees. This shows each element that makes up the gross pay and each deduction made before payment, and the amount of net pay.

8   Pay rises, bonuses and other rewards should always be paid on the date on which they are due. Again, it is a mark of respect and value.

9   Economic rent is the payment of very high rates for particular forms of expertise. While this is clearly essential in some circumstances, care is to be taken that the appearance of overpayment of some individuals is likely to have a detrimental and damaging effect on the rest of the workforce. Payment of high salaries which distorts the general pattern should only be contemplated when all other approaches have failed.

10 Payment of low rates is certainly possible for unskilled staff in periods

of high unemployment (e.g. the UK in the early 1990s). Again, this should only really be contemplated if there is no alternative – for example, if the organization is going through a lean time. Under-payment is a mark of contempt for the staff.

11 Pay freezes and reductions are also demoralizing and damaging to the staff. Again, they should only be contemplated when there is no other alternative.

Benefits

Benefits are items and services offered by employers to employees as part of the reward package. They consist of the following.

- *General benefits:* loans (for example, for season tickets), pension (con-tributory and non-contributory), subsidies (on company products, canteen, travel), car, telephone/car phone, private health care, train-ing and development, luncheon vouchers.
- *Flexible benefits:* packages that all staff members can have access to if they wish to do so and which are offered to all staff members on the same basis.
- *Chains of gold or super-benefits:* school holidays (teachers); cheap loans (banks, building societies); free/cheap travel (railways, shipping, air-lines); pension arrangements (for older and longer-serving staff).

The main reasons for using benefits are as follows.

- To encourage certain types of behaviour – for example, paying for training courses; paying subscriptions to professional associations and expert bodies; paying for accommodation while employees are working away from home.
- To encourage potential employees to join the organization – for example, relocation expenses, travel packages, use of company cars.
- As a way of retaining employees – for example, the opportunity to buy shares; increases in holiday entitlements in line with length of service; enhanced pension rights.
- The recognition of long service – for example, presentations after spe-cific time periods. As a demonstration of being a caring employer – for example, sick pay; occupational health schemes; life assurance; health insurance and private health care plans; school fee plans.
- A commitment to equal opportunities – for example, nurseries; career break schemes and sabbaticals; flexible hours and locations.
- To meet expectations; and to ensure that, as people's expectations rise, so do the benefits that accrue to them.

Flexible benefits may also be used as a means of recognizing and indicat-ing enhanced status – for example, allowing certain grades of employee to travel first class, stay in 4- and 5-star accommodation, providing high quality cars. However, this invariably detracts from the fundamental basis of equality that is essential to all flexible working arrangements.

In general therefore, benefit packages will be made available to staff on an even footing. The only exceptions are where the benefit is work-related to certain categories of employee; even in these circumstances, the offering of benefits to certain groups of employees but not others must be on operational grounds alone.

NOTES

1 *Choosing the benefits.* The mix of benefits available depends on the patterns of work of the employees and the nature of the organization's business. Some organizations do have hook-ups with others – for example, working for a travel agent entitles the opportunity of free travel on certain airlines, shipping and railway companies; some organizations provide discount cards for their staff to be used at department stores, supermarkets., travel agencies and finance companies.

   Benefit choice is most effective when things that are offered benefit all employees; where the ability to choose is based on personal and occupational circumstances; and where the benefits are not seen as privileges only available to a chosen few.

2 *Benefits and cash alternatives.* Some organizations allow their staff either to choose the benefit or to take a cash equivalent. For example, if it is not possible for an employee to use up their total annual leave allowance during the course of a year for operational reasons, then a cash alternative should always be made available. If it is not possible for a parent to bring their child into the company nursery, a cash payment should be made instead.

3 *Individual choice.* Giving individuals the choice of determining which benefits they require from a total package enables them to weigh up their own current needs and how their organization can best serve them. This reinforces the positive message that the organization cares about them as an individual as well as an employee.

4 *Chains of gold.* Chains of gold are extremely attractive to employees when they first come to work and as long as the relationship between employee and employer remains productive and positive. They become a burden on the individual when the relationship is lost. This is especially true where a financial commitment has been entered into as an integral part of the employment package – a free/cheap loan from a bank or building society; subscription to a pension or life assurance arrangement as part of a flexible benefit's plan. There is at least a moral duty on employers to make arrangements for as painless an arrangement as possible to be entered into when the employee seeks to leave the organization. In this way, the employee concerned is

looked after to the best of the organization's ability for the whole term of their employment. It also gives positive messages to those remaining in that they are reassured that if they do suddenly need to leave, they will be taken care of properly.

CONCLUSIONS   Motivating the flexible workforce is about creating the conditions necessary for high quality, productive, profitable and effective work to take place. This is only possible where a good environment is created and adequate equipment and technology are present.

In order to be able to maximize and optimize this, high quality staff have to be employed. A flexible work approach means that high quality staff are:

- positive and committed; highly trained; able to work in a range of different areas; able to use as much of their capability as is required;
- committed to continuous development and training; committed to the long-term future of the organization.

This in turn is only possible if there is top quality management and supervision. Top quality managers and supervisors are also highly trained and expert, highly committed, and highly motivated. They also take an active responsibility for the long-term and continued success of the organizations for which they work.

At an operational level, effective management of the flexible workforce lies in the ability to make each of the different components work effectively in particular situations. It also means recognizing and meeting the obligations to the staff. Above all, it means keeping in mind that the purpose of flexible working – indeed of all working – is to create top quality products and services which customers wish to buy and use, and which will encourage them to keep coming back for more.

Chapter 5

Staffing the flexible workforce

Human resource strategies and policies are designed and devised to meet the operations and undertakings of the organization. They reflect overall aspirations; business strategies and policies; direction; technology; skills, knowledge and expertise. They need to meet the aspirations of those who carry out the work. They address the formation of the required culture, attitudes, values and beliefs. They define the 'aura' and 'ethos' of the organization. They set out the desired type of employer and define the management style. They establish the standpoints to be taken on specific issues as follows. **INTRODUCTION**

- Work analysis and staff planning, recruitment, selection, assessment, succession and promotion.
- The style of human resource management to be adopted and fostered in the everyday dealings with and between staff. Industrial relations, representation, rules, regulations and procedures.
- The approach to the health and well-being of the employees.
- The approach to be taken to safety at the workplace.
- Employee development, work methods and practices.
- Pay, remuneration and benefits.
- Employee services, job analysis, design, improvement and enrichment.
- Personnel specification.
- Performance standards establishment, maintenance and appraisal.
- Human resource maintenance.
- Attention to discipline, grievance and disputes.
- The assumption of responsibility for ensuring levels of performance.
- The content of induction and orientation programmes.
- The basis on which opportunities are offered to individual employees.
- Evenness and fairness of treatment of employees across the entire organization, as well as within individual departments and functions.
- Health and safety and occupational health.
- Attention to work station design and improvement.
- Attention to work development, enhancement and enrichment.
- Attention to organization and staff development.

Figure 5.1

Human resource
management
summary

Area of work	Strategy and direction	Personnel operations
Work design and structuring	Principles, approaches, departmentalization, organization structure	Job descriptions, work patterns, work structuring
Staff planning	Systems appraisal, design commissioning	Systems usage
Recruitment and selection	Standpoint (grow your own, buy from outside)	Training of recruiters and selectors, recruitment and selection activities
Induction	Policy, content, priority	Delivery
Use of agencies and external sources of staff	Principles, circumstances	Contacts and commissions
Performance appraisal	Purpose, systems, design, principles, aims and objectives	Systems implementation, training of appraisers and appraisees
Pay and rewards	Policy, levels, mix of pay and benefits, package design	Assimilate individual staff to policy
Occupational health	Policy, content, design of package	Operation of package in conjunction with functional departments
Equality	Standards, policy, content, context, ethics	Policy operation, monitoring of standards, remedial actions
Industrial relations	Standpoints (conflict, conformist), representation	Negotiations, consultation, participation, staff communications
Discipline	Policy, procedure, practice, design, standpoint	Implementation of policy and procedure, support for staff, training of all staff
Grievance	Policy, procedure	Implementation of policy and procedure, training of all staff
Training and development	Priority and resources	Activities, opportunities, accessibility
Dismissal	Standards of conduct, examples of gross misconduct	Operation of disciplinary procedures, operation of dismissal procedures, support and advice

Human Resource Management is divided into strategic and directional
activities; and personnel activities. The role and function is:

policy, advisory, consultative, supporting, a point of reference; personnel
practitioner; establisher of policy content; establishing standards of best
practice; creator of personnel activities; monitor/evaluator of personnel
activities.

Equality of treatment, opportunity and access is an issue of attitude, or corporate state of mind. It is a fundamental prerequisite to the creation of organization and operation effectiveness. Managers and organizations must first overcome the tendency to compartmentalize people by race, gender, religion, marital status, disability, age, location, postal address, non-essential qualification, school background, club membership, hobby and interest, etc. They must take the opposite standpoint of isolating the qualities essential and desirable to carry out a job. They must view people in terms of their potential as staff members, as contributors to the success and prosperity of the organization. Without this, true equality of opportunity cannot exist.

EQUAL OPPORTUNITIES

There is also a question of basic human decency, that requires that all people be treated the same. This is a social as well as organizational concern. For organizations, all activities, management style, policies, practices and procedures, publications, advertisements, job and work descriptions, person specifications are written in ways that reinforce this. This emphasizes, formulates and underlines the required attitudes and beliefs.

These standards are based on operational capabilities alone. Anyone, including managers, adopting a negative approach or attitude to equality of opportunity or who victimizes, harasses or bullies members of their staff, must be subject to organization discipline.

Offering equality of opportunity to all sectors of the workforce is both cost-effective and profitable. By concentrating on (discriminating against) certain sectors of the population on operational grounds, organizations greatly limit their prospects either of making effective appointments or of maximizing the human resource.

The lead, therefore, comes from the top of organizations and the attitudes filtered down to all the staff. Organizational equal opportunities policies must be clear, unequivocal and easily understood by all concerned. They must be valued and adopted at all levels and in all sectors and departments. A genuine adoption of the principle of equality for all constitutes excellent marketing to the human resource of the organization. Staff are known to be valued for their capabilities. It also underlines any high moral or ethical stance taken in other business and organizational activities.

This is a dynamic and continuous process, of which all managers should have a good understanding. This is because of the increasing complexity of organizations and activities: legislation; the availability of required expertise; technological changes and advances; labour turnover patterns; the structure of the workforce; the changing nature of labour markets; imbalances between skills available and required; the nature of core and

STAFF PLANNING

peripheral workforces. All of this is increasingly an expected and integral part of the task of any manager in every functional area and activity (see Summary Box 5.1). The key elements involved are as follows:

1   *Work analysis* to order jobs and occupations in ways that are interesting, rewarding and fulfilling to the individual, and profitable and effective to the organization.

2   Assessing the *staff/manpower mix,* by each of, and a combination of, the following criteria: age; length of service; jobs held; promotions; sex, race, ethnic origin; skills and knowledge and expertise in different categories; flexibility and transferability.

3   The balance between the *supply* of labour, and *demand* for labour, overall, by location, and by the elements of the manpower mix given above; and the reconciliation of this supply and demand.

4   *Future projections* for staff, based on accurate and informed projections of business activity and the HRM activities that are implicit in this.

5   *Manpower information and computer systems,* and the information that they contain; managers are concerned not so much with the content and components of these systems as with the conclusions, use and value of the information.

6   *Constraints,* especially resource constraints and those imposed by budget considerations and other operational factors. These include location and any consequent implications for the nature and type of workforce; the history and traditions of industrial and commercial activity in the area in question; and operational constraints that may be imposed by ways of working and industrial relations agreements.

HIGH QUALITY STAFF This is the context and background for the recruitment, retention, motivation and development of high quality staff. High quality staff are either attracted from outside or produced and grown from within.

Outside

The benefit of recruiting from outside is to bring in fresh talent, skills, knowledge and expertise. Attitudes and behaviour are formed and developed at the commencement of employment.

Outsiders are also used to bring fresh life or impetus to existing activities.

Once inside, outsiders are trained and developed according to the organization's policies and practices.

The problems normally lie in the length of time the recruitment and selection processes take (several months for some appointments, especially management, technical and professional); and in the length of time

The view normally taken of staff planning and analysis is:

- to assess the balance between the supply of, and demand for, labour, skills qualities and expertise;
- to assess the workforce against specific criteria of: age; length of service; gender; disability; racial/ethnic origin; jobs held; promotions and transfers applied for and gained; skills knowledge and expertise ranges; succession and progression;
- to assess and project the likely and possible workforce requirements;
- to identify and analyze specific issues such as absenteeism, labour turnover, accidents, sickness, strikes, disputes and grievances;
- to retain both statutory and adequate information about all members of staff.

The flexible approach in many cases simply requires the broadest possible view of these factors. This should be based on:

- the fact that most people when given opportunities will take them, especially if they understand that it is in their best interests to do so;
- the fact that all people aspire to their own version of self-fulfilment (see elsewhere), and that work is an integral part of this;
- the fact that prescriptive, unvaried and routine work has a detrimental effect on morale, i.e. all work situations and occupations;
- taking an unrestricted and enlightened view of the talents and qualities of everyone in the workforce, whatever their current occupation; this means avoiding barriers that are often purely perceptual.

The results of effective staff planning and analysis is to enable a steady supply of effective, good quality, motivated staff; and to enable each member of staff to progress as far as their talents and commitment will carry them.

it takes to make them fully effective in their new roles (and this is the drive behind all effective induction programmes and activities). It is also essential that, as well as capabilities and expertise, attitudes and approaches are tested during the selection process. This is because in all aspects of flexible working these are of vital importance.

Growing your own

Growing your own means that organizations get the staff that they need and want. This extends especially to attitudes and behaviour. It greatly contributes to staff motivation. It is a mark of the value placed on the staff and the organization's commitment to them.

The main drawback is the length of time that this takes. Growing your own is a long-term and continuous commitment. It also tends to promote introspection and elitism if it does not include activities away from the organization (e.g. training and development courses off-site).

The best approach is clearly a mixture of the two. This is based on an understanding and evaluation of the specific benefits of growth and development and where the needs for fresh impetus lie. Emphasis is also needed on the integration of outsiders as quickly and effectively as possible.

Continuous improvement and development

This is a reflection of the required commitment to training and development. It covers improving the ways in which current activities are carried out. It also means reviewing, refining, streamlining and restructuring bureaucracy and administration where necessary. It also includes project work, work improvement activities, attention to quality, secondments and off-site activities, as well as on-the-job training.

Job titles

The great majority of job titles tend to limit and pigeonhole people into restrictive and restricted positions. They create inflexibility of themselves. Many job titles also demean the job holder, especially in semi-skilled and unskilled areas. For example, it is not unusual to hear people say 'I'm only a secretary' or 'I'm only a checkout operator' and if individuals themselves think that they are 'only' something, then the organization is likely to regard them in this way too.

This also happens to others elsewhere on organization maps and ladders. There is relative status accorded to and within personnel, marketing and finance functions for example, through the use of job titles such as 'Junior Personnel Officer', 'Finance Assistant' or 'Marketing Executive'.

As well as generally restricting this form of title, it tends to put a dampener on the enthusiasm of job holders and to indicate boundaries of responsibility, authority and activity which are not to be crossed.

There are also the pigeonholes for the un-pigeonholeable. At their most positive, titles such as 'Project Officer' or 'Manager of Corporate Affairs' tend to be allocated to those whose remits do not sit easily within an organization structure or hierarchy. This tends again to reinforce any general lack of flexibility. At its most negative (and much more common), is the tendency to use such titles for those for whom no real job exists. And nobody is fooled – not the rest of the organization, not the work colleagues and certainly not the job holder.

Some organizations have tried to get over this by introducing much more generic and (supposedly) positive titles such as 'crew member', 'cast member' or 'staff member'. Others have gone further still and allowed people to invent their own job titles. In the most extreme cases, this is fanciful and silly; but it does at least indicate that people are not to be bounded by restrictive job titles (see Summary Box 5.2).

SUMMARY
BOX 5.2

Fitting the
work to
people:
fitting the
people to
work

'Fitting the work to people/fitting the people to work' is a development of a more traditional approach that used to be known as 'Fitting the job to the man/fitting the man to the job'.

This requires an understanding of the critical elements of the work and the skills, knowledge, attributes, qualities, attitudes, behaviour, expertise, qualifications and experience necessary to carry it out. It requires an understanding of the kind of people who are likely to hold these qualities. It requires an understanding of the extremes of the job – those elements that are brilliant and attractive, and that consequently attract applications from people who wish only to carry out those parts of it; and those elements that are boring, dirty, dangerous; or else require personal displacement (for example, working away from home for long periods of time).

The purpose is to produce effective work definition so that people both capable and willing to carry it out can be matched to it. It is essential therefore, that it draws attention both to work attributes and also to wider elements such as work methods, style, environment, present and future opportunities and constraints.

From a management point of view, the main quality necessary is recognition that this should be done. It need not be long and complicated. It should not be neglected however. At its simplest it represents a quick checklist and aid to thinking. It also represents the first and most important step in the stucturing of flexible, dynamic and responsive workforces. If this first stage is not right, the rest of the process is also flawed.

Japanese companies tend to go along the line of promoting company identity (rather than job identity). Employees tend therefore to say 'I work for Mitsubishi' or 'I work for Honda' rather than 'I am a technician' or 'I am a supervisor'. This flexibility is borne out by operational practices which require the staff to work anywhere that the company requires and (at its best) removes the words 'That is not my job' from the employee's vocabulary.

The value of all this is as follows:

1   The ability to build a full and useful workforce profile using the criteria of: age; qualifications; capabilities and capacities; training and qualifications; full- and part-time job holding and patterns; subcontracted and networked arrangements; equal opportunity considerations of race, gender, disability and other non-statutory elements.

2   Establishing the right size of the organization: this includes up-sizing (taking on additional staff and devising new patterns of work); downsizing (including lay-offs, redeployments and redundances); and rightsizing (matching the size and scope of the workforce with the range of work to be done).

3   Skills and technological currency and obsolescence: including staff redevelopment and regeneration; organization redevelopment and regeneration; the creation of the necessary attitudes.

4   Skills matches and mismatches: including the ability to build skills, knowledge and experience profiles of the workforce; identifying matches, over-matches, under-matches and mismatches, and using this as the basis of informed effective remedial action and development strategies.

5   Turnover analysis: the ability to establish why people leave the organization and/or its component departments; the nature of these reasons, whether positive or negative; the extent to which those who move on, remain within or go outside the organization; the extent to which the reasons that people move on is inside or outside the control of managers.

6   Recruitment planning: including identifying the difficulties in recruiting particular types of staff; recognizing the problems, negative issues, bad (and perceived to be bad) job and operational features; identifying the attractions and positive aspects of the organization and its work both as a whole and also in particular departments and occupations.

7   Behaviour and expertise development, analysis and potential: the ability to recognize individual potential; the preparation of career paths and long-term productive and effective employment; the ability to identify negative patterns of behaviour on the part of groups and individuals; the ability to identify particular patterns of strikes, disputes, grievances, accidents and emergencies.

8   Succession: identifying the potential for individual and occupational careers within the organization; recognizing both the opportunities and limitations: the ability to offer variety, interest, changes of location, changes of project, changes of activity as well as promotion and more traditional career paths.

Job descriptions and person specifications

This reflects the ability to parcel up work on the one hand, and to match this with skills, qualities, attributes, capabilities and willingness on the other. Job descriptions and person specifications are different sides of the same coin. Under flexible working, job descriptions encompass and reconcile the following.

•   Organizational requirements of transferability and moveability – especially from quiet areas to those of heavy demand.
•   Personal requirements of job holders:
    a) to pursue the career or occupation with which they are concerned to which they are committed;

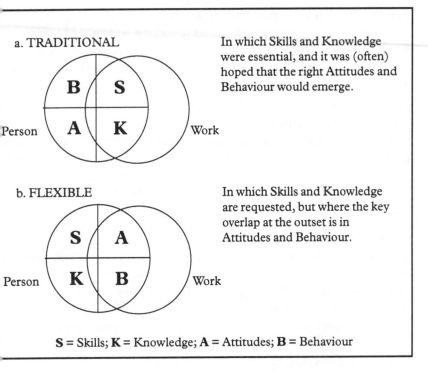

Figure 5.2

Fitting the work
to the person/
fitting the person
to the work

a. TRADITIONAL — In which Skills and Knowledge were essential, and it was (often) hoped that the right Attitudes and Behaviour would emerge.

B S
A K
Person / Work

b. FLEXIBLE — In which Skills and Knowledge are requested, but where the key overlap at the outset is in Attitudes and Behaviour.

S A
K B
Person / Work

S = Skills; **K** = Knowledge; **A** = Attitudes; **B** = Behaviour

b) ensuring that work is not too bitty or fragmented;

c) meeting personal expectations.

The ability of everyone to serve the organization and its customers, consumers and clients to the best of their ability.

To indicate (but not prescribe) a workload or occupational balance identifying main priorities and responsibilities, key results, output targets.

To ensure that scope is given to enable everybody concerned to work as necessary, desirable or required in pursuit of organizational aims and customer satisfaction.

To assume responsibility for every action taken in the name of the organization.

The standpoint taken is that everyone is to be prepared to do anything, at any time. Rather than itemizing tasks, the approach is to emphasize the need to 'work as directed' and 'work as required'.

This is shorter and more positive than the traditional method of itemizing each and every task that may be required of the job holder. It is much easier to understand. It is a better basis for a positive, productive and effective working relationship. It is also far less bureaucratic. It places on managers and supervisors the responsibility for organizing and directing work from a positive and meaningful point of view.

In cases where it is necessary to emphasize or indicate the range of work to be carried out, a list of tasks is added to the end of the description. There will also always be the rider that this list is not exhaustive and may be added to or changed at any time by agreement and with consultation.

The result is to greatly reduce the number of job titles and especially those that tend to limit or demean (see above). While what is put in their place is not necessarily perfect either, it at least shows an inherent value and respect for the staff. It also shows the high level of trust and integrity necessary in the working relationship – if people are to be genuinely required to take responsibility for their actions, management style must itself be supportive, positive and based on absolute trust and integrity.

Person specifications

The person specification is a statement of the qualities and expertise required. In flexible working, the emphasis is on positive attitudes, a willingness to learn and develop, dynamism and responsiveness, as well as skill and capability. 'Want to do' and 'Will do' become as important as 'Can do'. There are also related qualities of creativity, innovation and interest.

It is quite legitimate to ask for these in job advertisements as well as indicating particular qualifications, skills and knowledge content. Those who genuinely hold these qualities are normally in great demand. They expect to be able to use these qualities in this kind of work, and do not stay long where they are not in fact required.

Skills and knowledge

Testing for skills and knowledge is carried out through:

- aptitude tests, from which the ability to carry out particular tasks or expertise can be inferred;
- skills tests, for example testing keyboard skills, data manipulation, presentation skills;
- specific techniques, for example lifting, proof-reading, design;
- quiz-type tests on capabilities that ought to be present as the result of having a specific qualification.

Attitudes and enthusiasm

Testing for attitudes and enthusiasm is carried out through:

- personality tests, which indicate these qualities;
- problem-solving tests, in which the attitude (as well as the solution) to the problem is observed;
- establishing the reasons why the individual wants to come and work for the company;

- participation in group discussions established for the purpose;
- in-tray exercises and 'work under pressure tests', which again enable the attitude (as well as the approach) to be observed;
- inferences from a person's general demeanour.

NOTES

1   Organizations that continue to use traditional and well-understood job titles must recognize that job holders will expect their work content to continue to reflect these. 'Manager' implies some form of executive responsibility. 'Secretary' implies typing, administration, filing and some office practice. If the work is to be very different from this, then the job title should be changed so that potential employees know where they stand from the outset.
2   If there are bad or boring activities, then these should be made clear at the outset and should be shared around as far as possible. Flexibility is not an excuse to dump all the bad bits on a new starter.

Selection

Selection concentrates on the key qualities identified in the person specification. The emphasis of any selection activities will be geared towards the identification of the required attitudes as much as the skill, knowledge and expertise. The view taken is that an effective flexible worker is a combination of expertise and attitude rather than a person with the highest level of expertise. In these circumstances, it is invariably better to take on someone who can do the job *and who wants to do it* than someone who is clearly an expert in the area but cannot always be bothered.

Induction

Successful flexible working is dependent upon effective induction. The required attitudes and values are reinforced during the induction period. Emphasis is also placed on getting the employee to carry out their expertise *in the ways required.* The length of induction, its priority, the attention paid to it by managers and supervisors – as well as the content of the induction programme – are all critical to its successful outcome. The main thrust again, is to build the foundations for the working relationship of the future (see Summary Box 5.3).

This is important for all staff whatever their jobs and work. Some organizations neglect the induction of part-time and unskilled staff because they are 'only' part-time and unskilled – and so again, the message given is the 'only'. There is no real chance of a fully productive relationship. Others neglect the induction of management, technological and administrative staff on the grounds that anyone with these skills and expertise should be able to find their own way into the job. This is also a negative approach. At the very best it takes longer to build up an effective working relationship. At the worst, it is alienating and destructive. Those affected will take refuge in their expertise, rather than building identity with the organization and their colleagues.

None of this means taking a long time over induction. It does mean using the time available to best effect. It means identifying and concentrating on those things that are important to the individual – any individual – at the outset of any employment – identity, familiarity and early achievement (see Figure 5.3). Those things that are important to the organization – positive attitudes, willingness to work – stem from this, and will follow once the others are right.

For all staff, whatever their location or pattern of working, frequency of attendance, or hours of work, the following is essential:

- beginning the development of a positive and productive working relationship with the supervisor or manager, and establishing the ways in which this is to be conducted;
- familiarization with the environment, procedures and practices;
- meeting work colleagues and building the occupational network, personal relationships, mutual trust and confidence;
- developing the required attitudes and values, standards of behaviour and performance;
- putting right any initial misperceptions or misunderstandings.

Time and trouble taken at the outset prevent misunderstandings occurring later. Where problems do subsequently occur, they are not then the result of anything that could have been put right earlier or prevented from happening altogether.

TRAINING AND DEVELOPMENT

Organizations that want flexible working must be prepared to train their staff initially regularly and continuously. Employees coming into flexible working situations must be prepared to undertake training on the same basis. This applies to everyone, at all levels of authority, skill and responsibility; and whatever their occupational duration, hours or patterns of work.

Training and development represents a mutual obligation – the obligation of the organization to see that all its staff are regularly and continuously trained, developed and updated; and the obligation of the individual to take responsibility for the skills, knowledge, capabilities and expertise necessary to secure their own future. Three points of view may be identified as follows.

- *Professional/occupation:* the development of the distinctive expertise and capabilities necessary to maintain and pursue designated lines of work.

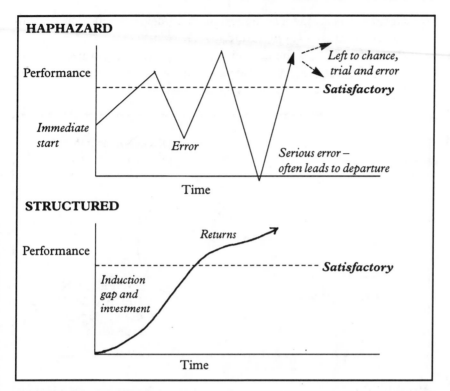

Figure 5.3
Induction
learning curves

Another way of looking at the results of induction – good or bad – is as follows.

- *Uncertainty:* whereby as the result of induction, the individual is uncertain of what is expected of them in their work for the organization.
- *Indifference:* whereby the individual is neither motivated nor demotivated as the result.
- *Alienation:* whereby the process has clearly gone seriously wrong and the individual sets out to move on again as quickly as possible.
- *Acquiescence:* whereby the individual will at least put up with the work that they are to do.
- *Conformity:* whereby the individual goes along with the standards and practices of the organization because it is in their best interests to do so at the present.
- *Internalization:* whereby the individual accepts the standards and values of the organization as absolute and builds the rest of their life around them.
- *Identity:* whereby a mutual identity is created between individual and organization for the duration of the working relationship.

For flexible working, the last – identity – is the most desirable. Genuine mutual identity is founded on confidence, trust, honesty, openness and integrity; and this reinforces the points made elsewhere about the necessity for a distinctive managerial approach and form of management and supervisory style.

SUMMARY BOX 5.3

Induction: the results of induction

- *Organizational:* undertaking training and development necessary to secure the organization's future.
- *Personal:* reflecting the acceptance of responsibility for training and developing for the future, and personal choice and preference for the future. The three are not always easily reconciled.

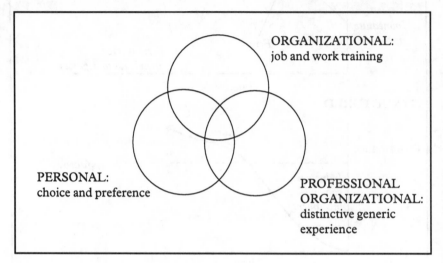

Figure 5.4

Training and development: the professional/ organizational/ personal mix

Production

Production staff are trained in all the necessary aspects – each work station, every part of the process from input of raw materials to output of finished goods. It also includes how to put right minor breakages and stoppages. It must include a quick and easily accessible point of reference to get repairs carried out when the machinery breaks down – and the authority to do this.

It includes training for the future to identify and develop potential, to prepare for new technologies that are likely to come along.

Service

For service staff, the approach is similar. This normally includes customer service and public relations skills. It also invariably includes the understanding and usage of information and communications technology.

Again, there are elements of training for the future in both technology advances and service improvements.

NOTES

1 For all these, there are elements of responsibility, the formation of positive, dynamic and committed attitudes.

2 Some production companies have abolished quality control functions altogether. Customer complaints are referred back directly to the team or individual which produced the item in question. The onus and responsibility is placed on each team or individual to avoid these problems so that they are not faced with customer complaints. Any further problem will be referred to a senior level of management who will then question them also.

3 Restaurant chains have begun to abolish the jobs of restaurant managers, head waiters, restaurant cashiers and restaurant purchasing officers at each of their locations. The scheduling and arrangement of tables is worked out among the waiters and waitresses and one of these will also take responsibility for cashing up at the end of the day before they all go home. The purchasing of food is carried out by the chef. The purchasing and ordering of drink is carried out by the bar staff. This results in enhanced job interest, job satisfaction, use and development of potential – and earnings. It has also meant attention to extensive job training and continued development of those involved.

4 Qualifications. Some organizations provide the means for some of their staff to pursue qualifications. Others provide this for all staff. Others still insist that their people study something – whether directly work-related or not. These qualifications may be at any level, from basic, professional, technical and business skills (at GNVQ Levels 1 and 2 for example), through to release for Masters' Degrees and Diplomas at universities and colleges.

   Whatever the level, distinctive improvements and enlargements of expertise are achieved. It also acts as a vehicle for unlocking potential and enthusiasm and generating much higher levels of expectation and performance all round.

   Some companies have had their in-house training programmes put on a formalized basis leading to recognized qualifications at the end. Completion of these is compulsory and a condition of continuing employment.

   Some companies pay for evening classes – again, whether work-related or not. They take the view that any development and any participation in organized activities is better than none. It also demonstrates the organization's wider general interest in their people.

INDUSTRIAL RELATIONS

Industrial relations – or employee relations, employment relations, staff relations, staff management – is the system by which workplace activities are regulated, the arrangement by which the owners, managers and staff of organizations come together to provide the means to engage in productive activity. It concerns setting standards and promoting consensus; it is also about the management of conflict.

Three distinct approaches may be identified:

- *Pluralism:* admitting a variety of objectives, not all compatible, among the staff. Recognizing that conflict is therefore present, rules, procedures and systems are established to manage it and limit its influence as far as possible.
- *Unitarism:* which assumes that the objectives of all involved are the same, or at least compatible, and concerned only with the well-being of the organization and its products, services, clients and customers.
- *Radicalism:* the view that commercial and industrial harmony is impossible until the staff control the means of production and benefit from the generation of wealth.

The first duty of management in managing workplace industrial relations is to recognize and understand which of these points of view is to be adopted. This is then translated into an industrial relations position as follows:

- *Conflict:* the basis on which staff are to be dealt with is one of mistrust, divergence, irreconcilable aims and objectives; in these cases, the industrial relations strategy will serve to contain the conflicts and to reconcile differences and to promote levels of harmony as far as possible.
- *Conformity:* where the diversity of staff and technology may be (and often is) extremely complex: but where the IR strategy rather sets standards of behavioural and operational aims and objectives that in turn, require the different groups to rise above their inherent differences.
- *Consensus:* where the way of working is devised as a genuine partnership between the organization and its staff (and their representatives, including trade unions). The consensus position in industrial relations is rare in all but the simplest and smallest of organizations (and often does not exist even in these).
- *Participation:* whereby the active involvement of staff in the setting and maintenance of standards is engaged: this may be reinforced through profit-sharing and company share ownership schemes.

Whichever point of view is adopted must be supportive of and complementary to the wider aims and objectives of the organization. Part of the agenda is also set by the capabilities, qualities, professionalism and expertise of the workforce. Ultimately however, the needs of the workforce must at least be reconciled, if not completely harmonized, with those of the organization. The following issues must always be covered:

- Establishing and regulating the standards of performance required.
- Establishing and regulating the standards of ethics, behaviour and attitude.
- Procedures for the management of disputes, grievances, discipline and dismissal.
- Consultative, participative and communication structures and methods.

- Precise forms of workforce/staff representation (including the recognition of trade unions).
- The desired general aura of workplace staff relations: the aura is reflected in the nature and number of accidents, disputes and absences; it may also be indicated by rates of labour turnover, problems with particular staff categories, problems with staff at different locations or on different work patterns; it is also a reflection of the organization culture.
- The structure of the workforce: operational aspects; dispersion/closeness; departmentalization and groupings; particular ways of working.
- Staff management aspects: of core and peripheral work groups; specialist subcontractors, consultants and advisers; those on permanent contracts; those on fixed-term/fixed project contracts.
- Balancing and reconciling a great mixture of conflicting and divergent elements in the basic interests of organizing and maintaining effective working methods; balancing harmony and contentment with commitment, drive and organization purpose.
- Establishing standards and sanctions for the enforcement of rules.
- The capability of managers: ensuring that managers and supervisors have the distinctive skills and qualities necessary for the effective management of industrial relations in the particular situation.

Industrial relations and flexible working

Because of the high quality of management necessary for effective flexible working, and the specific levels of behaviour and attitudes required, the approach to industrial relations is usually conformist. Conformist industrial relations requires the subordination of divergent and conflicting interests in the pursuit of common and understood organizational aims. These are set in advance of any staff agreement and work practices. The position normally adopted is that the organization must be successful, effective and profitable, and that the purpose of industrial relations (like all other workplace activities) is to contribute to this.

For the approach to be truly effective, obligations overwhelmingly rest with the organization and its managers. Standards are preset and prescribed and not the subject of negotiation. Areas of managerial prerogative, matters for consultation and aspects that are open to negotiation are all clearly stated. Conformism leaves much open to consultation but very little to genuine negotiation. Above all, collective bargaining and other instruments and procedures for the containment of conflict are not normally present in flexible working situations.

There are procedures however, and these are quick and direct. Managers seek to solve problems and promote harmony. Conflicts of interest between groups are kept to a minimum. Disputes, especially those concerning pay and conditions, are resolved within given deadlines. Staff identity with the organization must be strong. The position of trade unions (and any other staff representative body such as staff associations) is clearly defined and limited at the outset.

Genuine participation is likely to be limited to profit-sharing and share ownership schemes in flexible working arrangements. The main exceptions to this are likely to arise in fledgling companies and those with very few employees; in these cases, participation may extend also into decision-making and business and organization strategy.

Whether industrial relations is to be conducted with or without the presence of trade unions, the reasons why people join trade unions must be removed. Trade unions grew to prominence in organizations to represent the employee's interests, to serve particular groups and as a brake on the worst excesses of management that led to a quality of treatment across the whole of the business sphere that, by any standards, commercial or ethical, was unacceptable and untenable.

This normally consists of adopting a benevolent, consultative and open mode of general communications, corporate attitudes to the staff and an enlightened general attitude as the cornerstone of the industrial relations and staff management approach. Operation of procedures and practices must be fair and perceived as such. Pay, pay rises, working conditions and other operational matters are consulted upon through works councils, staff associations and other communication fora.

Responsibility for the style and tone of industrial relations rests entirely with the organization. Staff adopt the desired corporate attitudes, value and aspirations. Trade unions (if there are any) operate within this framework.

Single status

The concept of single status is based on an ethical stance that all employees are to be treated equally and that the same fundamental terms and conditions of employment are to apply to all. Terms and conditions, and elements of the contract of employment on such matters as holiday accrual, hours of work, provision of staff facilities, working clothes and safety and protective wear, are the same for all. Participation in such things as profit related pay or merit award placement schemes involves everyone.

Behavioural issues reinforce this. Everyone is addressed in the same manner regardless of occupation. The work of each employee is valued and respected; differentiation between groups and categories of employees is on the basis of work function only: there are no exclusive canteens or car parking spaces.

Human resource management in flexible working situations and arrangements is to create the basis of an harmonious productive working environment so that effective work can be carried out. In those industries and organizations where moves towards full workforce flexibility have been made, this approach is familiar and understood. Human resource management is recognized as a business activity, a key function that contributes both to the effectiveness and the profitability of the organization. What matters therefore, is not so much the existence of each of the elements of human resource management (these are more or less universal) but the ways in which these are carried out.

Above all, it is essential that there is a full and continuing commitment to the development of all employees. As the value of this becomes more widely recognized and the benefits can be seen to translate into increased profits, service quality and organization stability, so the profile and priority of these activities will rise.

It is also essential that whatever the past history and tradition of industrial relations, there are now fresh and new ways of carrying out these activities that must be understood and implemented. Much of this has been pioneered by Japanese companies establishing workplaces in the UK and elsewhere in Western Europe for the first time; at the same time, indigenous companies such as Body Shop, Marks & Spencer and Rentokil have come to very similar conclusions from their own particular perspective. In each of these cases, the common denominator is fully flexible working; and this, together with the fact that they have all survived and grown during the recession of the past ten years, makes them excellent examples to follow.

CONCLUSIONS

Chapter 6

Management and the flexible workforce

The first duty of all organizations in managing flexible working is to get the right attitudes and approaches of its managers and supervisors. Where flexibility is based on part-time fixed-term contracts and job sharing type work, the approach that demeans – 'They are only part-timers' and 'They are only job-sharers' – is unacceptable. It is absolutely certain that if people are treated as 'only' something, this is how they will turn out. Work, profitability, productivity, effectiveness and customer service are all certain to suffer. Moreover, this attitude is certain to spread to other full-time staff who will regard themselves as superior. It will then spread to part-timers who are likely to develop some form of siege mentality. They are certain to develop defensive and negative attitudes. The result again, is to affect effectiveness and profitability.

All employees, whatever their hours of work or length of service, are to be treated fairly and equally. Any departure from this line is punished. Any failure to do this is certain to result in grievances, court and industrial tribunal cases which are all costly and debilitating.

The management task is therefore to produce excellent and top quality staff who make excellent products and give high levels of service. This is the source of customer satisfaction, repeat business, enhanced reputation – and profits. Flexibility is designed to underpin this – it is not an excuse to ignore it.

MANAGEMENT STYLE Flexible working is best supported by an open, honest and visible style of management and supervision. This is especially important where large numbers of part-time staff are present and where people move around regularly between different tasks during the work periods. Visibility builds the trust and empathy essential in any effective working relationship. For part-timers and those who do move around, this has to be built quickly (see Summary Box 6.1).

Honesty and openness are also critical. Very often, there is an organizational issue at stake. The organization itself must first learn the difference between being open and not – and the benefits of the former and the drawbacks of the latter. In many cases, organizations lose sight of the reasons why certain things are kept confidential. While confidentiality

'When I took over Semco from my father, it was a traditional company in every respect with a pyramid structure and a rule for every contingency. Today, our factory workers sometimes set their own production quotas and even come in in their own time to meet them without prodding from management or over-time pay. They help redesign the products they make and formulate the marketing plans. Their bosses, for their part, can run our business units with extraordinary freedom, determining business strategy without interference from the top brass. They even set their own salaries with no strings. Then again, everyone will know what they are since all financial information at Semco is openly discussed. Our workers have unlimited access to our books (and we only keep one set). To show we are serious about this, Semco, with the labour unions that represent our workers, developed a course to teach everyone, including messengers and cleaning people, to read balance sheets and cashflow statements.

'We don't have receptionists. We don't think that they are necessary. We don't have secretaries either, or personal assistants. We don't believe in cluttering the payroll with ungratifying, dead-end jobs. Everyone at Semco, even top managers, fetch guests, stand over photocopiers, send faxes, type letters and use the phone. We have stripped away the unnecessary perks and privileges that feed the ego but hurt the balance sheet and distract everyone from the crucial corporate tasks of making, selling, billing and collecting.

'One sales manager sits in the reception area reading the newspaper hour after hour, not even making a pretence of looking busy. Most modern managers would not tolerate it. But when a Semco pump on an oil tanker on the other side of the world fails and millions of gallons of oil are about to spill into the sea, he springs into action. He knows everything there is to know about our pumps and how to fix them. That's when he earns his salary. No one cares if he doesn't look busy the rest of the time.

'We are not the only company to experiment with participative management. It's become a fad. But so many efforts at workplace democracy are just so much hot air.

'The rewards have already been substantial. We have taken a company that was moribund and made it thrive, chiefly by refusing to squander our greatest resource, our people. Semco has grown six-fold despite withering recessions, staggering inflation and chaotic national economic policy. Productivity has increased nearly seven-fold. Profits have risen five-fold. And we have had periods of up to 14 months in which not one worker has left us. We have a backlog of more than 2,000 job applications, hundreds from people who say that they would take any job just to be at Semco. In a poll of recent college graduates conducted by a leading Brazilian magazine, 25% of the men and 13% of the women said Semco was the company at which they most wanted to work.

'Not long ago, the wife of one of our workers came to see a member of our human resources staff. She was puzzled about her husband's behaviour. He was not his usual grumpy autocratic self. The woman was worried. What, she wondered, were we doing to her husband?

'We realized that as Semco had changed for the better, he had too.'

From Ricardo Semler: *Maverick* – Free Press (1993)

clearly extends to customer bases and profiles, new products, services and initiatives and other operational brainwaves, there is very little else that needs this approach. The more that is kept from the staff, the more they conclude that the organization is hiding something.

A substantial part of the management job consists therefore of 'walking the job'. Where this is not possible – for example, where employees work from home or in regional centres – regular and positive telephone contacts are to be maintained. This should be supported by regular meetings.

Regular meetings are also essential where there is a large measure of contact through e-mail and fax. This breaks down physical and psychological barriers and enhances identity.

The priority is attention to operational requirements and the patterns of staffing necessary to make these effective.

Administration and procedures are to be kept as simple as possible. There is an administrative workload generated by the variety of work terms indicated and used. This is accommodated by standardizing and simplifying as much as possible, especially forms of contract of employment and work procedures. Use and adherence to procedures is kept to a minimum, reserved for serious issues only. Smaller problems and issues are resolved by the work group, managers and supervisors on the spot. This frees up both time and resources for the primary purpose of pursuing customer satisfaction and product and service excellence. It also removes the need for industrial relations, staff management and other administrative superstructures and subfunctions; and this again frees up resources for more positive and productive purposes.

Procedures for the handling of disciplinary and grievance matters should be kept as simple as possible. They should be used as infrequently as possible – because managers and supervisors have the capability of resolving issues before recourse to procedures is necessary. Where it is necessary to invoke procedures, strict time constraints should be imposed. This prevents issues from festering, from people taking sides, from battle lines being drawn. The purpose is to get operations back on a successful and effective footing as quickly as possible. The vast majority of grievances will be resolved on the spot. Where procedures are invoked, this should take no longer than two weeks.

Disciplinary matters should follow the same pattern. The only constraint is to allow the employee time to prepare their response to an issue and to seek representation and support for their point of view. This is also the approach for reporting relationships between departments and senior management.

Information required and provided should be suitable and effective. Continuous attention should be paid to the volumes and quality of information available, and the purposes to which it is put.

egular requirements – for example, for year end – are clearly signalled
nd structured into departmental workloads. Information systems
ould be designed and commissioned with the demands and require-
ents in mind in order to eliminate crisis requests, overloads and
nderloads.

ter-departmental relations and relationships between operational and
nior management are based on organizational effectiveness rather than
dherence to procedures. Problems that do arise are to be resolved
uickly and effectively, again with the emphasis on product and service
uality and customer satisfaction.

here the issues concern staff, procedures must be followed and these
e to be kept simple and effective (see Summary Box 6.2).

or flexible working the following qualities are essential:

**MANAGEMENT
QUALITIES**

Enthusiasm, commitment, dedication.

Regular positive access between manager and staff member by telephone.

Regular personal access in the interests of building mutual confidence and satisfaction in the particular situation.

Visibility.

The capability and willingness to address and resolve problems and
issues quickly and positively.

Quick and effective decision-making capabilities.

Understanding and supporting the needs and demands of staff,
whatever their pattern or location of work.

Knowledge and understanding of the pressures, opportunities, constraints and drives present in the workplace; of those that can and
cannot be controlled; of other constraints in which work is to be carried out.

Knowing and understanding what constitutes successful and effective performance; the ability to take remedial action quickly when
performance falls short; handling staff, production, service and customer problems when they arise.

Adopting a style of management leadership based on the 'leader' column in Summary Box 6.2; and adopting the point of view that the
qualities exhibited in the right-hand column headed 'Non-leader' are
unacceptable and not to be tolerated.

nother way of looking at this is to adopt the point of view that the man-
ger or supervisor of a flexible workforce or work group is their ultimate
upporter and servant. A research team working at the European Busi-
ess School at Fontainebleau, France, in 1989 proposed two leadership
nd management models supportive of this (see Figures 6.1 and 6.2).

SUMMARY BOX 6.2

Leadership

Peters and Austin (1986) identified a long and comprehensive list of factors present in a 'leader': and they contrasted this with the mirror attributes of the 'non-leader'.

Leader	*Non-leader*
Carries water for people.	Presides over the mess.
Open-door problem-solver, advice-giver, cheerleader.	Invisible, gives orders to staff, expects them to be carried out.
Comfortable with people in their workplaces.	Uncomfortable with people.
No reserved parking place, dining room or lift.	Reserved parking place and dining table.
Manages by walking about.	Invisible.
Arrives early, stays late.	In late, usually leaves on time.
Common touch.	Strained with 'inferior' groups of staff.
Good listener.	Good talker.
Available.	Hard to reach.
Fair.	Unfair.
Decisive.	Uses committees.
Humble.	Arrogant.
Tough, confronts nasty problems.	Elusive, the 'artful dodger'.
Persistent.	Vacillates.
Simplifies.	Complicates.
Tolerant.	Intolerant.
Knows people's names.	Doesn't know people's names.
Has strong convictions.	Sways with the wind.
Trusts people.	Trusts only words and numbers on paper.
Delegates whole important jobs.	Keeps all final decisions.
Spends as little time as possible with outside directors.	Spends a lot of time massaging outside directors.
Wants anonymity for himself, publicity for the company.	Wants publicity for himself.
Often takes the blame.	Looks for scapegoats.
Gives credit to others.	Takes credit.
Gives honest, frequent feedback.	Amasses information.
Knows when and how to discipline people.	Ducks unpleasant tasks.
Has respect for all people.	Has contempt for all people.
Knows the business and the kind of people who make it tick.	Knows the business only in terms of what it can do for him.
Honest under pressure.	Equivocation.

Looks for controls to abolish.	Looks for new controls and procedures.
Prefers discussion rather than written reports.	Prefers long reports.
Straightforward.	Tricky, manipulative.
Openness.	Secrecy.
As little paperwork as possible.	As much paperwork as possible.
Promotes from within.	Looks outside the organization.
Keeps his promises.	Doesn't keep his promises.
Plain office and facilities.	Lavish office, expensive facilities and furnishings.
Organization is top of the agenda.	Self is top of the agenda.
Sees mistakes as learning opportunities and the opportunity to develop.	Sees mistakes as punishable offences and the means of scapegoating.

Peters and Austin add the following two riders to their version of these columns:

- 'You now know more about leaders and leadership than all the combined graduate business schools in America.'
- 'You also know whether you have a leader or a non-leader in your manager's office.'

From Peters and Austin: *A Passion for Excellence: The Leadership Difference*, Harper and Row (1986).

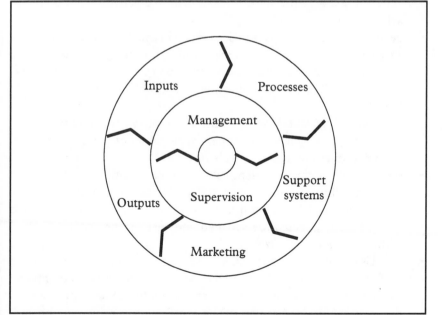

Figure 6.1

The circle: in which organizational activity is seen as an unbroken continuum of which management is simply a part.

Figure 6.2

The inverse pyramid: in which the manager or supervisor is placed at the bottom point, prima facie supporting and serving the workforce rather than sitting on top of it.

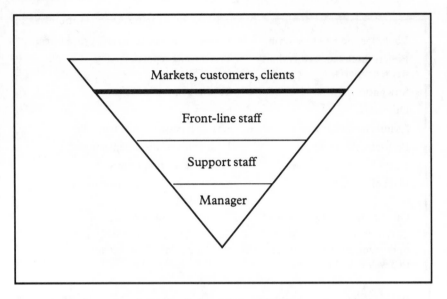

MANAGEMENT TRAINING

Training in the skills and qualities needed to manage the flexible workforce consists of:

- setting performance standards and getting these across quickly and effectively; devising ways in which these are best supported according to the demands of a particular situation;
- ensuring that managers and supervisors have positive attitudes and dispositions towards their staff; ensuring that managers and supervisors understand what constitutes customer satisfaction and expectations and the nature and quality of activities necessary to achieve this;
- developing interpersonal skills, as much of the supervision and management routines are concerned with promoting understanding; harmonizing persons on a variety of working arrangements; consultation and briefings; solving questions and problems without recourse to procedures;
- developing high standards of communication, written and spoken;
- developing managerial and supervisory habits of 'walking the job' (also known as managing by walking about);
- training in practical problem-solving in all activities – product and service quality, customer issues, staff and personal matters and questions. The emphasis is on quick and effective solutions with which those directly affected are satisfied and that can be accommodated within the wider organization;
- appraisal, knowledge and skills, based on continuous assessment of performance with regular formal or semi-formal punctuation marks. Regular staff appraisals need not and should not take long; most of the work is best done as part of the continuous working relationship.

Again, problems become apparent early and are easily nipped in the bud. This is especially essential when managing part-timers and out-workers with whom regular face-to-face contact is limited. It is damaging to both production, quality and morale if issues are allowed to drag on without being resolved;

- discipline and grievance based on establishing and maintaining standards of working relationships that keep both to a minimum. Management and supervisory training in these areas is concerned with equipping those involved with the capabilities and autonomy to resolve issues before they become problems. Providing training in the operation of simple, direct and speedy procedures indicated elsewhere is in the context of maintaining staff morale and effectiveness;

- training in staff management and people management – including interpersonal skills, assertiveness, developing positive attitudes, developing workforce and workplace harmony; fostering team spirit and genuine identity;

- developing the work group as a professional, motivated and high quality entity; attending to work and operational development needs; attending to professional and personal training and development; ensuring the rejuvenation and regeneration of the group; ensuring its constant development; ensuring that when new members of staff come in, they are integrated as quickly and effectively as possible (see Summary Box 6.3);

- organizing working time so that flexible workers and out-workers get real access and identity and the opportunity to build full personal, professional and operational relationships; continuous regular briefings concerning organizational, departmental, divisional, group and individual performance with the emphasis on the positive and the early identification and resolution of problems;

- knowledge and understanding of all aspects of organizational operations and activities; where the individual manager or supervisor fits in; the nature of their required contribution; familiarity with the work of related departments; understanding required performance targets: understanding the constraints within which they have to work.

Management training and development is a continuous requirement. Some is clearly best pursued in-house. The pursuit of external courses and formal qualifications is also highly desirable because it broadens the general perspective and understanding of managers; it enables them to come into contact with others from other organizations, bringing fresh ideas to bear on existing issues and problems; and develops the fund, knowledge and talent available in the organization.

SUMMARY BOX 6.3

The summer job

Keith Roberts is an undergraduate student at Bristol University. He has taken a summer job at the biggest factory in his home town in the Midlands. On the first day, he was told to report to the warehouse supervisor. The supervisor assigned him to a small group of men who were responsible for loading and unloading the lorries that supplied the materials and carried away the finished goods of the factory.

After two weeks at work, Keith was amazed at how little work the rest of the crew accomplished. It seemed that they were forever standing around and talking, or in some cases, even going off to hide when there was work to be done. The result was that Keith often found himself alone unloading the lorry while the other members of the crew were messing around, having tea breaks or simply absenting themselves. When Keith complained about this to the other workers they made it very plain that if he did not like it, he should leave: but if he complained to the supervisor, he would be sorry. He was also excluded from any of the rest of the workers' activities such as taking tea and lunch breaks together or having a beer on Friday nights together at the pub across the street. One day, he went up to one of the older members of the group and said 'What on earth is the matter with you people? I'm just trying to do my job. I'm only here for the summer. The money is good. I will be leaving to go back to university in a few weeks' time. I wish I could have got to know you all better; but I am actually very, very glad that I am not like you at all.'

The older member of the crew replied 'My friend, if you had been here as long as I have you would be just like us.'

This is an archetype of the traditional inflexible industrial situation. It illustrates the need for management awareness, capacity and willingness – and therefore, training – in each of the areas indicated in the text; and especially:

- setting and maintaining standards for everybody – and this includes supervision as well as the work group;

- the need to integrate and treat with equality, respect and value all members of the group, whatever the period of time they are being employed for;

- the extremely destructive effects of negative attitudes and non-performance.

Source: F. Luthans – *Organizational Behaviour:* McGraw Hill (1990)

MANAGEMENT PERFORMANCE

Effective management of flexible working requires high quality and distinctive forms of expertise, based on the style indicated above and for which initial and continuous training is required. The manager or supervisor is the point of reference for all staff – whatever their length of service, level of expertise or hours worked. Their people look to them for quick and effective decisions, solutions to problems, and the creation of an effective, positive and productive place of work.

The elements of managerial performance are:

- setting and maintaining the required attitudes and values, reinforcing these through personal conduct and performance and remedying these where they fall short;
- setting goals, aims and objectives for the department or division as a whole and for teams, groups and individuals within it;
- delegating, giving autonomy, authority and responsibilities to subordinates to complete work as they see fit;
- enabling and supporting the pursuit of projects and initiatives;
- improving and developing the expertise of all staff;
- controlling the work and performance of persons on a variety of different expertise, experience, hours and patterns of work;
- acting as advocate and spokesperson for the department and its members;
- being receptive, evaluative and judgemental of ideas received from members of staff;
- continuously seeking for improvements to product and service quality; and for improvements to work methods and practices;
- involvement in and involving the staff in the choice of new production technology, work methods and practices;
- enhancing the department's recognition and achievement.

Effective flexible work management is dependent upon individual managers and supervisors having the capabilities and qualities to carry this out (see Summary Box 6.4).

CONCLUSIONS

Effective management of flexible working – in whatever form – depends upon understanding the psychological and behavioural needs of those being managed. Assuming that the organization has got everything else right – it has invested in the necessary technology; it has taken the strongly supportive attitudes necessary in all types of flexible working; and that it has hired people with the right expertise and attitudes to do the work – the key to maintaining this, enhancing and improving it, lies un ensuring that the people continue to be both capable and willing. Continuing capability is dealt with through the presence of continuous training and development, and participation in this will be compulsory.

Ultimately therefore, management style is concerned with maintaining the willingness of people to continue to work effectively and productively under whatever circumstances necessary. This is only achieved by paying attention to the factors indicated in this chapter and above all, those aspects of flexibility, openness, honesty and integrity on the part of managers. In all forms of flexible working, management tasks and priorities have to be reordered so that workforce and individual support is of

SUMMARY BOX 6.4

Alienation

Alienation is the term used to describe feelings such as the following:

1 Powerlessness: the inability to influence work conditions, work volume, quality, speed and direction.

2 Meaninglessness: the inability to recognize the individual contribution made to the total output of work.

3 Isolation, which may be either physical or psychological. The physical factors arise from work organization requiring that people are located in ways that allow for little human interaction and feelings of mutual identity and interest. The psychological factors are influenced by the physical. They also include psychological distance from supervisors, management and the rest of the organization.

4 Low feelings of self-esteem and self-worth arising from the lack of value (real or perceived) placed on staff by the organization and its managers.

5 Loss of identity with the organization and its work, the inability to say with pride 'I work for organization X.' This is reinforced by the physical and personal commitment made by the individual to the organization in terms of time, skill and effort and which does not bring with it the psychological rewards.

6 Lack of prospects, change or advancement for the future: feelings of being stuck or trapped in a situation purely for economic gain.

7 General rejection: based on adversarial, managerial and supervisory styles and lack of meaningful communications, participation and involvement. This is increased by physical factors such as poor working conditions and environment.

8 Lack of equality, especially where the organization is seen or perceived to differentiate between different types and grades of staff to the benefit of some and detriment of others.

Alienation is the major fundamental cause of conflicts and disputes at places of work. It is potentially present in all work situations. Those who design and construct organizations need to be aware of it in their own particular situations and to take steps to ensure that ideally it can be eliminated or at least kept to a minimum and its effects offset by other advantages.

In flexible working arrangements, alienation is potentially very easily enhanced by the patterns of attendance (e.g. for part-time staff) and working away from the organization and in isolation for long periods (e.g. with sales staff and home workers). In these cases, each of the points indicated above become major issues and they affect motivation, morale – and quality of output.

They are only addressed effectively through an organizational commitment to the managerial style indicated earlier in the chapter; and in ensuring that managers understand the consequences of not following this line of approach.

paramount importance. Management training and development must be continuous and constantly directed towards a greater understanding of this. The returns are to be seen in the excellence, effectiveness, high quality productivity – and profitability – of the work carried out by the staff. Failure to do this is certain to result in each of these elements being diminished.

Chapter 7

Flexible working in practice

It is clear by now that flexibility and flexible working come from an attitude, a culture, a corporate state of mind: much more can be achieved by people who are prepared, willing and able to do more than by people placed in straitjacketed, formalized job descriptions and work patterns outside which they never stray.

ORGANIZATION STRUCTURE AND FORMS

There are two factors:

* creating flexible, enhanced and improved working practices in existing organizational formats;
* creating new organizational forms.

Existing organizational forms

This refers to the enhancement of work and working practices in bureaucracies (both multinational and public service), multinational head offices and divisionalized structures and formats, holding companies, and agglomerates (for example, the Korean Chaebol and Japanese Keiretsu). This form of organization is certain to continue to dominate both commercial and public services for the foreseeable future. The concern is therefore to get the best out of the existing arrangements – and this means attention to quality assurance and work improvement programmes; induction, initial and continuous job training; creating the desired attitudes of flexibility and responsiveness; enhancing the value that every employee brings to an organization; and concentrating on ensuring that procedures and bureaucratic forms work in the interests of the organization and its customers and clients (rather than being an end in themselves). The priority given to project teams, work improvement groups and quality circles has to be enhanced. It is also essential to recognize the problems caused through working across national boundaries and in different cultures, and in taking steps to remedy these either by granting measures of autonomy to those in particular locations, or through the creation of speedy and effective communications between those in the field and head office (see Summary Box 7.1).

The concept of quality circles was American and post-war in origin. It was exported to Japan which, in turn, made it an integral part of the continuous quality improvement process in organizations. A quality circle is a group of staff which meets on a regular basis to review the whole area of quality at the workplace. This involves identifying and clarifying problems, selecting issues from among these for resolution, organizing and prioritizing them, setting deadlines, timetables and target dates, and setting aims and objectives by which the improvements in the quality of the organization's operations can be measured. To be effective, they require accommodation, resourcing and support from the organization and a commitment to back the judgements of the quality circle. Organizations have to recognize that there is a pay-back, not only in improvement in quality or, at least, in problem identification, but that this is also instrumental in promoting the desired attributes of greater commitment, achievement, identity and participation by all concerned. Quality circles are voluntary, generating and selecting their own leadership, frequency and timing of meetings, and precise agenda format. Where they have worked, especially in Japanese companies, it has been because there is a greater cultural pressure to participate, together with an environment created that is both conducive to, and expectant of, a full measure of involvement (whether something is actually designated voluntarily or not).

New forms of organization

Core and peripheral organizaions

These forms of structure are based on a total reappraisal of objectives and activities with the view to establishing where the strategic core lies, what is needed to sustain this, and where, when and why additional support and resources are required.

The essential is the core. The rest is the peripheral and may be seen as a shamrock or propeller. This is seen as:

- Professional and technical services and expertise, drawn in to solve problems; designed and improved work methods and practices; manage, change and act as catalysts and agents for change. All of these functions are conducted by outsiders on a contracted basis. Areas include marketing, public relations, human resource management, industrial relations, supplies, research and development, process and operations management and distribution.
- Sub-contracting of services such as facilities and environment management, maintenance, catering, cleaning and security. These are distinctive expertises in their own right, and therefore best left to expert organizations.

   This form of subcontracting is now very highly developed across all sectors and all parts of the world as organizations seek to concentrate on their given expertise and minimize areas of non-contributory activity.

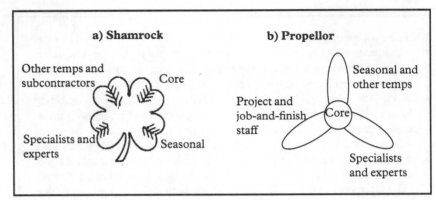

a) Shamrock b) Propellor

- Operational pressures, in which staff are retained to be available at peaks (daily, periodical or seasonal) and otherwise not present. This has contributed to both the increase in part-time, flexible and core hours patterns of employment; and also to the retention of the services of workforce agencies, who specialize in providing particular volumes of expertise in this way.
- Outworking (often home-working), in which staff work at alternative locations including home, avoiding the need for expensive and extensive corporate facilities. This also enables those involved to combine work with other activities – parenting, study, working for other organizations.

For this, people may be paid a retainer to ensure their continued obligation and loyalty. They may be well paid, even overpaid, to compensate for periods when there is no work. They may be retained on regular and distinctive patterns of employment – normally short-time or part-time.

The benefits lie in the need and ability to maximize resources and optimize staff utilization. Rather than structuring the workforce to be available generally, the requirement for expertise and nature of operations is worked out in advance and the organization structured from this point of view. All activities that are to be carried out on a steady-state daily basis are integrated into the core. The rest are contracted or retained in one of the forms indicated.

Federations

Federations are extensions of the core and peripheral format. It tends to be more or less regularized between organizations with their own specialisms which are then harmonized and integrated in the pursuit of overall stated objectives. Within this, each organization has its distinctive identity and full autonomy to pursue and conduct other work as long as it meets its obligations and makes its contribution to the federation.

The main problem lies in integrating, co-ordinating and controlling the relationships and activities required of each contributor. The critical factors are ensuring mutuality of interest, continuity of general relationship, communications and harmony. The reporting relationship is based on a combination of work contract (or contract for services) and measures of integrity, rather than on a bureaucratic or legal/rational format.

Operationally, the critical factors are meeting volume and quality requirements and deadlines. A much simpler and clearer form of direction and purpose is likely to emerge as the result and this is focused on performance overall rather than procedures and functions.

The likelihood is therefore that organizations will seek to simplify all of their features as they become involved in this form of activity. As well as clarifying purpose, it also frees up resources that otherwise have to be used in accommodating staff and their equipment, supporting rules and procedures and the sub-functions that operate them.

A simple definition of organization culture is: *the ways in which things are done here.*   **CULTURE**

Culture is formed from the collection of traditions, values, policies, beliefs and attitudes that prevail throughout the organization.

The following elements are always present:

- *History and tradition:* the origins of the organization; the aims and objectives of the first owners and managers; their philosophy and values; the regard in which these are currently held; the ways in which these have developed.
- *Nature of activities:* historical and traditional; current and envisaged.
- *Technology:* the relationship between technology and the workforce, work design, organization and structure; alienative factors and steps taken to get over these; levels of technological stability and change; levels of expertise, stability and change.
- *Past, present and future:* the importance of the past in relation to current and proposed activities; special pressures (especially struggles and glories) of the past; the extent to which the organization is living in the past, present or future; the pressures and constraints that are brought about as the result.
- *Purposes, priorities and attention:* in relation to performance, staff, customers, the community and environment; and to progress and development.
- *Size:* structure; formalization; rules and procedures. Larger organizations are much more likely to have a proliferation of divisions, supervisory structures, reporting relationships, rules, processes and procedures; there is therefore a much greater propensity for communication difficulties, interdepartmental rivalries and problems with co-ordination and control.
- *Location and locations:* geographical location and locations; the constraints and opportunities afforded through choosing to be, for

example, in urban centres, at the edge of town, in rural areas; working in domestic and foreign markets; working in old and new markets.

- *Specific social pressures:* strong social, ethical and religious customs that are present in the workforce and locations of work.
- *Management style:* the stance adopted by the organization in managing and supervising its people; the stance required by the people of managers and supervisors; the general relationships between people and organizations and the nature of superior-subordinate relations.

This is the basis of organization culture. Furthermore, the best organizations design their culture. This involves setting the standards of attitudes, values, behaviour and belief that everyone is required to subscribe to as a condition of joining the organization – and these attitudes and values must be capable of acceptance and internalization on the part of those who do join the organization. Policies are produced so that everyone knows where they stand, and these are underpinned by extensive induction and orientation programmes and training schemes. Procedures and sanctions exist to ensure that these standards continue to be met. Organizations with designed cultures are not all things to all people – many, indeed, make a virtue of their particular approach of 'many are called but few are chosen'.

This is in contrast to where the culture is emergent – formed by the staff (and staff groups) rather than directed by the organization. The result is that people think, believe and act according to the pressures and priorities of their peers. They pursue their own agenda. This is clearly fraught with difficulties and dangers: organizations that allow this to happen, succeed only if the aims and objectives of the staff happen to coincide absolutely with their own. Emergent cultures tend to create canteen cultures; elites and cliques; realpolitik; and over-mighty subjects and departments.

Creating a culture of flexibility, dynamism, improvement and responsiveness depends upon attention to the following:

- Recognizing that culture is learned rather than genetic or biological.
- Recognizing that culture is shared: and that therefore the attitudes and values must be capable of acceptance.
- Continuity: cumulative in its development and passed on from one generation to the next.
- Integrated: changes in one area will lead to changes in others.
- Adaptive: based on human qualities of adaptability, creativity, innovation and imagination.
- Regular: when participants interact with each other, they use common language terminology, and recognized and accepted forms of behaviour.
- Dominant values: advocated by the organization and expected by participants.
- Norms: establishing distinctive standards and patterns of behaviour.
- Rules: formal rules underlining the constitution of the organization; informal rules governing the interaction of individuals on a daily basis.

- Organizational climate: conveyed by the environment, the physical layout, the ways in which participants interact and the relationships with the outside world.
- Rewards: the ability to reward those working in the organization according to their own needs, wants and expectations.
- Reputation: internal reputation of departments and divisions; external reputation of the organization in its wider environment.
- Legal constraints: recognizing and working within the legal restrictions of the particular location/sector/industry/public service.
- Ethical: setting distinctive standards of practice and performance in relation to staff, customers, clients and community.

Specific pressures must also be recognized as follows:

1   The interaction between the desired culture, and the organization's structures and systems. Serious misfit between these leads to stress and frustration and also to customer dissatisfaction and staff demotivation.
2   The expectations and aspirations of staff; the extent to which these are realistic; and can be satisfied within the organization. This becomes a serious issue when the nature of organization changes and prevailing expectations can no longer be accommodated. Problems also arise when the organization makes promises that it cannot keep.
3   Management and supervisory style, the extent to which this is supportive, suitable to the purpose and generally acceptable to the staff.
4   The qualities and expertise of the staff, the extent to which this divides their loyalties. Many staff groups have professional and trade union memberships, continuous professional development requirements and career expectations, as well as holding down positions and carrying out tasks within organizations. In many cases – and especially when general dissatisfaction is present – people tend to take refuge in their profession or occupation, or their trade union.
5   Technology and the extent to which it impacts on the ways in which work is designed, structured and carried out.
6   Working customs, traditions and practices including restrictive practices, work divisions, specialization and allocation, unionization and other means of representation; and the attitudes and approaches adopted by both organization and staff towards each other – flexible and co-operative, adversarial, degrees of openness.
7   The extent to which continuity of employment is feasible; or conversely, uncertainties around future prospects for work and employment. This includes degrees of flexibility, the extent and prevalence of employee and skills development, learning sub-cultures and the wider attitude of both staff and the organization to this. It also affects reward packages.
8   Internal approaches and attitudes to the legal and ethical issues indicated, the extent of genuine commitment to equality of opportunity

and access for all staff; whether or not different grades have different values placed on them, standards of dealings with staff, customers, communities, suppliers and distributors.

9   The presence of pride and commitment in the organization, its work and its reputation; standards of general well-being; the extent of mutual respect.

10 Communication methods and systems, the nature of language used, the presence/absence of hidden agenda.

11 Physical and psychological distance between functions, departments, divisions and positions in the organization and its hierarchies.

CONDITIONS   Flexible working requires the right conditions. Creating these is a matter of organizational policy and strategy. It requires long-term and continuous investment in premises, technology, the working environment and, above all, the staff. The paybacks are in continuous profits, successes and effectiveness – measured especially over the longer term (see Summary Box 7.2).

SUPERVISION   Flexible working requires a distinctive type of day-to-day management and supervision. Managers and supervisors work close to the staff, as well as with the production targets, procedures and systems. To make this humanly possible, the procedures and systems are kept as simple as possible so that time and resources are released for primary purposes.

Managers and supervisors are highly trained and skilled. They have a set of priorities based on customer satisfaction and product/service quality. This in turn is only possible if high quality staff are engaged (see Summary Box 7.3).

HIGH QUALITY STAFF   High quality staff are highly flexible, skilled and trained; highly motivated and committed; and as well paid as possible (see Summary Box 7.4). They share in organizational profits and successes. They participate in development. They also participate in mistakes and failures which are put right from a positive point of view of learning and development.

High quality staff are ready, willing and able to do whatever is required in the organization's best interests. They must be highly motivated as well as highly skilled. This comes about as the result of:

•   transformation in customer expectations: already brought on by, for example, 24-hour banking; extended shop opening hours; extended office opening hours; and the increasing perception that, if any one organization in a particular sector can do this, then so can/should all the others;

•   the need to be able to deal with suppliers, distributors, customers and clients on a 24-hour basis;

In the early 1990s, a large manufacturing company in the north-west of England sought to introduce various methods of work improvement. This included total quality management, full multi-skilling and the abandonment of the distinction between full-time and part-time staff. It called the initiative its 'Quality Improvement Programme' (QuIP). It put a middle manager in charge of the programme part-time. The first that staff knew about this was when a memo landed on their desks telling them that this was indeed in place.

The company set up a steering group to examine particular areas of work, but no members of senior management were involved. The group members each served six months on a full-time basis. Line managers and supervisors 'volunteered' members of staff that they could do without for half a year. The group therefore had poor calibre members. Members of the group knew that they had only been sent because their supervisors wanted them out of their way. Everyone else in the organization also knew this.

Steering group members were given a lot of training and spent much of their period away on courses. Others whose potential had (supposedly) been identified were given a lot of training but the training was never used and most people never put it into practice. People were trained on technology and quality assurance matters that were never introduced.

The result was inevitably that the 'QuIP' initiative folded. Some members of the steering group went back to new posts. Others left the organization. Managers and supervisors who had sent people to the steering group realized that they could do without them. Some were made redundant. Others were relocated – either at their own or the company's volition. The initiative therefore, fell quickly into disrepute. The lessons to be drawn from this are:

- the establishment of long-term aims and objectives;
- the establishment of adequate continuing levels of investment;
- ensuring that senior management is fully committed and involved from the outset;
- steering groups should be given executive responsibilities and real 'teeth';
- organizations must be serious about their involvement and committed to any results that are produced;
- managers given direct responsibility for the introduction of such programmes must have full executive authority;
- such projects must be managed by full-time (not part-time) co-ordinators;
- training and development must be relevant to people's jobs and capable of being put into practice;
- consequences of this form of failure must be recognized – in future, it will be that much harder for the organization to get similar initiatives off the ground.

SUMMARY BOX 7.2

The flexible work project that failed

SUMMARY BOX 7.3

Delayering and flexibility

A critical part of the development of flexible working and top quality staff is the giving of extended responsibility and authority as well as improving and enhancing skills and knowledge.

The result of this is to reduce the need for hierarchies and layers of supervision; and to reduce the need for large numbers of managers and supervisors. Several different approaches have been taken.

Walmart

Walmart Inc. is the largest supermarket chain in the world. Founded by Sam Walton in 1946 it has grown from being a single store operation to having a presence in every State of the United States and many other parts of North America. It currently has 950 stores.

The head office establishment is exactly that which first ran the original operation. Extensive autonomy, responsibility and authority (and high levels of pay and reward) are given to store managers. At head office nobody has their own desk, secretary or any other trappings of status that give rise to psychological distance.

Virgin

The Virgin Group was founded by Richard Branson in 1969. Originally a single second-hand record shop, it has grown over 30 years to become: a music and recording empire; a major retailer and distributor; an airline; a travel and tour operator; and railway franchisee.

The company is run from a Thames barge moored at Chelsea in London. This is the company's head office and it has a staff of eight. Again, everything else is devolved to the operating units.

ABB

ABB (Asea Brown Boveri) was a traditional bureaucratic Swedish engineering multinational. It was transformed by the efforts of Percy Barnevik when he became Chief Executive in 1989.

Barnevik took the view that the bureaucratic structure and processes necessary to gain executive decisions were contributing directly to increased levels of cost, slow and cumbersome decision-making processes and bad communications.

The company was restructured into autonomous divisions and subgroups numbering no more than 150. Barnevik's original plan was to reduce the grouping sizes to no more than 50. However, this was not feasible because of some of the technology used on specific projects.

Each group leader was given extensive executive responsibility, authority and autonomy and required to report to head office only when there were major insurmountable problems or when matters arose that were outside their control. The establishment at head office was reduced from 2,000 to 220.

Nike

The Nike company expressed its concerns for the future as follows: 'Unless new employees are capable of assimilating Nike expectations of centred hard work and caring creative thought, Nike will stagger under the weight of a jet-setting, self-centred, arrogant – and average – middle management who aggrandize themselves on a past they were not a part of instead of striving for future successes in which they can share.'

Japanese organizations working in the UK and elsewhere in Western Europe and North America set their pay and reward levels right at the top end of the particular sector in relation to domestic operators in the same field.

Thus for example:

- Nissan, Toyota and Honda pay higher wages than Ford and Vauxhall in the UK;
- Sharp, Sony, Panasonic and Toshiba pay higher wages than Pye, Ferguson and Philips;

and the Japanese companies also offer full job security. In return, the staff have to accept full flexibility of working.

Body Shop

The Body Shop pay their staff above the average for the retail sector. They do not pay their staff the best wages in the retail sector. In addition however, they offer a clear and distinctive identity with the company; and part of this identity means accepting and internalizing the distinctive ethical values of the organization's founders. All Body Shop staff are required to work one day per month on community or environmental projects. Part of the reward here is therefore in terms of a (perceived) contribution to society and the wider environment.

- attention to the issues raised by engaging in different patterns of working;
- understanding the priorities and demands of staff of different types and levels of expertise;
- establishing a series of priorities for the management of high quality and effective staff;
- creating work patterns that operate in everyone's best interests;
- managing work patterns so that these operate in everyone's best interests;
- creating a basis, environment and structure for work groups that accommodate all the divergent pressures (see Summary Box 7.5);
- understanding the pressures brought about by different patterns of working and attendance;
- understanding the problems brought about by different patterns of organization structure – this is especially true where there is extensive outsourcing and subcontraction and where 'just-in-time' methods of supply and delivery are engaged (see Summary Box 7.6);
- creating a basic set of values based on positivism and equality; this, above all else, gets over problems inherent in designating people as full-time, part-time home-workers, occasional hours, agency and temporary staff – all of which are potentially divisive;

SUMMARY BOX 7.5

___

Effective work groups

All groups have their own entity, life and distinctive existence. They have their own core values, reasons for belonging and commonality and universality of purpose. The basis of all effective groups is mutual trust, honesty, openness and understanding.

Groups and their leaders are responsible for the following:

- *Management of the task:* setting work methods, timescales, resource gathering, problem-solving and maintenance functions.
- *Management of the process:* the use of interpersonal skills and qualities, and the interaction with the environment to gain the maximum contribution from each member.
- *Managing communications:* between different work groups, disciplines and professions; within different work groups, disciplines and professions.
- *Managing the individual:* making constructive use of individual differences and talents, and ensuring that each contribution is both valued and of value.
- *Management style:* the creation and adoption of a style that is both positive, dynamic and suitable to the needs of the situation.
- *Group maintenance:* ensuring that administration and support services are available and suitable to the needs of the group.
- *Common aims and objectives:* that are understood, valued and adopted by all members, and that are the overriding common purpose for being in the situation.
- *Shared values:* the standards of behaviour and attitudes that all members of the group can agree to and in which they have confidence and belief, and with which they can work.
- *Group and team spirit:* a combination of the shared values, ethics and ethos of the group or team concerned and the extent of the positive identity and loyalty that the members have to each other, to the tasks in hand and to the overall objectives; while its positive contribution to performance is not always fully realized or evaluated, the negative effects of the destruction of group identity and team spirit are often devastating. Group and team spirit are founded on a combination of mutual confidence, trust, respect and value; and early and continuing work/group achievement.

Each of these features must be present, whatever the work method or pattern adopted and whatever the nature of the task in hand. Lack of a sense of belonging or group identity leads to demotivation, alienation – and a downturn in results, quality of products and services. *This is, therefore, a key feature in the management of all effective flexible working situations.*

The following views may be taken of this as follows.

1. Value chain

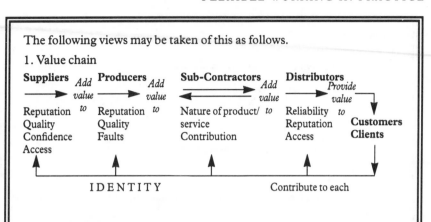

2. Supply chain

3. Perceptual barriers

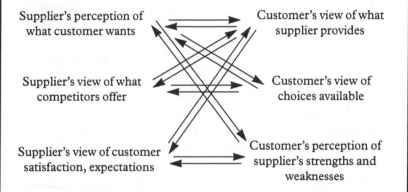

The common factor in each case is the management of the relationships that exist between different organizations. The key to this form of effective flexible working is the ability to: recognize and understand the problems that are inherent; and establish a sufficient quality of personal and professional relationships to overcome the potential blockages and barriers.

SUMMARY BOX 7.7

The work/ quality/ rewards equation

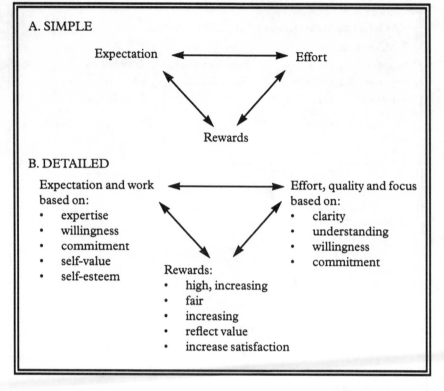

A. SIMPLE

Expectation ⟷ Effort

Rewards

B. DETAILED

Expectation and work based on:
- expertise
- willingness
- commitment
- self-value
- self-esteem

⟷

Effort, quality and focus based on:
- clarity
- understanding
- willingness
- commitment

Rewards:
- high, increasing
- fair
- increasing
- reflect value
- increase satisfaction

- engaging the high quality and levels of work for high rewards equation (see Summary Box 7.7);
- recognizing the relationship between expectation, effort and reward, and harmonizing these as far as possible;
- removing from the working environment those things that tend to demotivate, especially adversarial and distant, managerial and supervisory styles, differentials based on status and elitism, and uncertainties in communications;
- recognizing the competitive edge that the flexible approach gives; recognizing that it is a continuous process that product quality, service levels and staff performance can always be improved.

The onus is on the organization and its managers to get their part right. As long as this is done, they have the right to expect the staff to work in the ways directed. This is supported by a positive and effective style of management; simple procedures; effective job and work design; attention to selection; and flexible contracts of employment. Potential levels of motivation in flexible working are very high and the conditions for these must be created by management.

Operations management

The management of operations and activities is driven by creating conditions where problems are kept to a minimum. This comes about first and foremost by understanding the nature of work demanded, the type of working environment and the opportunities and constraints presented. All of this indicates where problems are certain or likely to arise. Steps can then be taken to minimize their effects. Where this is not possible, compensations, variety, enhancement and enrichment have to be offered for best results. In the longer term, this indicates needs for work technology and environment redesign. In the shorter term, there is a pressure on managers and supervisors to monitor the effectiveness of work and the working environment, to identify issues as they arise and to take whatever steps necessary to minimize their effects (see Summary Box 7.8).

Joan Woodward first identified archetype scales of production as the result of studies carried out in Essex in the late 1950s. They remain current and valid at present and are:

- *unit:* the production of single items in response to specific customer requests;
- *batch:* the production of specialist and/or short run volumes of products and services:
- *mass:* the production of universal consumer goods on a large scale;
- *flow:* the production of oil, petrol, chemicals, plastics, iron and steel on a continuous process.

The distinctions between each, while remaining apparent, are becoming ever-more blurred. The following should be noted.

- Batch and mass production technology is itself becoming ever-more flexible, both in terms of what it can be retuned and rejigged to produce, and also in terms of the speed at which it can be operated.
- Mass and batch product quality is under ever-increasing pressure to be provided: customers, consumers and clients take the view that, if high levels of product quality are available from unit producers, they should be available everywhere.
- Customers, consumers and clients have ever-greater choice and are therefore less disposed than ever to wait for the particular product of their choice unless they have their own overwhelming personal reasons for doing so – the pressure is therefore on mass and batch producers to get products to market as quickly as possible.
- The refinery and extrusion technologies that are used in flow production are themselves subject to ever-advancing improvements, both in response to the continuing drive to maximize returns on investment and also because of ever-greater consumer demand.
- Customers, consumers and clients expect ever-increasing levels of service as well as the product itself. This applies to all types and levels of production. It also applies whether the 'product' is a tangible item or intangible service (see Figure 7.1).

**SUMMARY
BOX 7.8**

**Joan
Woodward
and scales of
production**

Figure 7.2

Product and ser-
vice relationships

The following forms of product and service relationship are available and have to be managed.

1. Product-only relationship

Key features are:
- primacy of product, e.g. energy and water supplies;
- primacy of core service, e.g. education and other statutory services;
- product exclusivity;
- demand outstrips supply;
- monopoly position of producer.

2. Product and service relationship

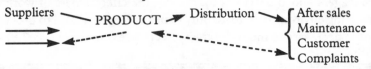

Key relationships are with suppliers and (if used) distributors.
Key features are: flexibility of supplies
speed of response in dealings with after-sales.

3. Total service relationship

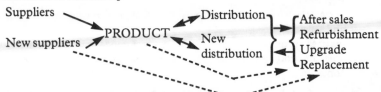

4. Relationship management

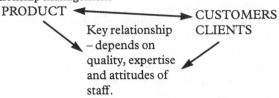

Notes
1   Product-only arrangements are completely dependent upon either a) product necessity (e.g. gas, electricity, water); b) supreme levels of product quality (e.g. branded goods); c) product exclusivity (e.g. perfume, Rolls Royce cars), if some form of service element is not necessary or required.
2   Total service provision and enduring service provision are themselves likely to depend on subcontracted, outsourced work as necessary and 'just-in-time' arrangements for their continued success.

There are therefore clear long-term obligations placed on organizations and their managers, to train staff to recognize and understand the importance and value of each of these relationships, and to service them accordingly.

Problem-solving

The approach to problems when they do arise is to nip them in the bud. This is a key contribution of visible and positive styles of management and supervision. Speedy and effective responses to all staff matters is essential. This keeps discipline, grievance and dismissal to a minimum. Poor or falling levels of performance and behaviour are picked up and rectified early. This is essential, especially for those who work away from the organization, and those whose hours are short or attendance infrequent. Putting people through disciplinary and grievance procedures is kept to a minimum and only used where all else has failed. It reduces administration and frees up resources for productive, effective – and profitable – activities. Where procedures are engaged they are operated as quickly as possible. Natural justice, fairness and reasonableness must be adhered to, but none of these are ever excuses for being dilatory or for institutionalizing problems. This also applies to customer complaints.

It is essential to recognize the following:

- customers can get *some* complaints resolved quickly and to their total satisfaction – they therefore expect *all* complaints to be resolved quickly and to their total satisfaction;
- if they do not get their complaint resolved quickly and to their total satisfaction, they will take their custom elsewhere;
- if an issue is important enough to a customer to make a complaint it is worthy of being treated with respect and courtesy by the organization to whom the complaint is being made.

From the organization's point of view, customer complaints should be seen as follows:

- the inability to solve a minor problem may cause the customer to take their major business elsewhere – for example, supermarkets have long taken the view that it is better to replace a faulty item (and in some cases also offer money back) than to lose a customer who may spend a lot of money each time they visit;
- customer complaints and quality assurance departments are expensive – it is therefore better to have the customer refer their complaint directly back to the person who made the product or offered the service in the first place:
- it is much better for organizations to admit their mistakes (when they have made them) and to replace the item or service in question, than to engage in protracted arguments with customers (the only person who ever wins such an argument is the customer).

The main issue is, therefore, the ability to get quickly to the heart of the problem and to resolve the matter to the satisfaction of the customer. Again therefore, a part of fully flexible working lies in the capability of all staff to identify, resolve and address such issues to the satisfaction of the customer.

Communications

Communications are simple and direct, and of high quality. The best approach again is the visible, underpinned by a fundamental soundness and integrity of working relationship and by clear and unambiguous documentation, written in the language of the receiver. This applies to all communications, whether they are produced for internal or external consumption. Quality, clarity and directness of communication are essential in the development of positive, harmonious and enduring staff relationships, customer relationships and relationships with the wider community and environment.

CONCLUSIONS   Flexibility requires a fundamental shift of traditional organizational approaches, from the rigid and hierarchical, to the pursuit of product and service quality and excellence. This is supported by high quality human relations, high levels of attention to product and service, an understanding of what constitutes customer satisfaction. It enables a much greater opportunity for products and services to be offered to customers and more scope for business development. It enables sectors of society to have job and work opportunities where these would not otherwise exist. It enables organizations to have access to much greater pools of capability, expertise, talent and potential than would otherwise be possible.

Flexibility paradoxically is conformist. It is based on high and distinctive standards of behaviour, attitude, performance and commitment. Those who work in flexible organizations accept these – or do not work. If they are to be effective and successful, they must be capable of harmonizing staff and organization, of finding and developing mutuality of interest in the working situation. In flexible working, there is no room for inflexibility or extensive procedural systems. There is no room either for cosy little jobs or long-term steady-state unchanging patterns of work or occupations.

Above all, it is an opportunity – for business to transform its activities and service quality; for public services to get to grips with often very limited resources; for managers to develop real management (as opposed to administrative and procedural) expertise; for customers to extend their range of choice and opportunity; and for staff – for people from all walks of life – to realize their potential, pursue interests and lead varied, productive and rewarding working lives.

Appendix A

Employment law in the UK: the legal framework

The sources of employment law are the same as all other legal areas:

- *Statute law:* defined by acts of parliament.
- *Criminal law:* consisting of offences against the nation or the Crown.
- *Civil law:* allowing for the resolution of disputes between individuals.
- *Precedent:* in which a judgement on one case is held to apply to others of a similar nature.
- *Custom and practice:* in which legal status is accorded to something that has gone on for a period of time.
- *European law:* the ultimate point of reference for any UK citizen on any legal matter including employment.

For employment law there are additional factors.

Fairness and reasonableness

All organizations are unique and because they vary so greatly the test of what is fair and reasonable in particular sets of circumstances is always applied. Fairness and reasonableness is based on a combination of:

- the size of the organization, the resources at its command and disposal;
- the nature of business and activities, the technology and equipment used, commercial and operational pressures;
- the nature of people employed, their skills, knowledge qualities and expertise;
- ways of working, including interpersonal relationships;
- respect, value and esteem for staff and customers, honesty and integrity, and ordinary common decency;
- specific legal standards (for example, health and safety, product quality and description, trading standards).

Fairness and reasonableness applies to conduct, behaviour and performance; and to both employers and employees.

Natural justice

Quite apart from any legal obligation, natural justice demands that people are treated equally and fairly and with respect and honesty in all walks of life; and work (or indeed lack of it) plays a significant part in everyone's life.

Best practice

Standards of staff and human resource management set by ACAS, the Department for Employment and expert bodies such as the Institute of Management and the Institute of Personnel and Development establish what is known as best practice. Best practice is a combination of fairness and reasonableness, honesty and integrity, natural justice, together with the operational ways of organizing and directing people in order to optimize organizational performance.

Precedent

Tribunal cases are treated as distinctive and individual and therefore on their own merits. Tribunal judgements do not set precedent. Precedent is only set in employment law cases where these are referred on or pursued beyond the EAT and into the mainstream judicial system.

AREAS COVERED BY EMPLOYMENT LAW

Contract of employment

This is the basis of the relationship between employer and employee. Not later than two months after starting work, any employee who works more than eight hours per week must receive a written statement giving:

- the name of the employer and the employee;
- the date when the employment began, taking account of any period of employment with a previous employer which counts as continuous with the present;
- pay or the method of calculating it, and payment interval;
- terms and conditions relating to hours of work, holiday entitlement, other time off including public holidays and holiday pay;
- job title or brief description of job;
- place of work or places along with the employer's address.

This is the principal statement and must be contained in one document. In addition, the following information must also be given or be reasonably accessible to the employee:

- terms and conditions relating to sickness, injury and sick pay;
- any pension arrangements;
- the length of notice the employee must give and receive;
- the period of employment, if it is temporary or fixed term;
- particulars of any collective agreements by which the employee is to be bound;
- any specific conditions that apply when the employee is to work outside the UK for more than one month;

- any disciplinary rules applicable to the employee and the person to whom employees can apply if dissatisfied with a disciplinary decision or if they have a grievance about their employment and the procedure to be followed.

Information given in job advertisements, job descriptions or other company information may also constitute part of the contract of employment.

Any change to the written particulars must be consulted on and agreed, and notified in writing to employees individually within one month of the change. If there is any dispute about the written statement either the employer or the employee may refer the matter to an industrial tribunal.

Collective agreements

This refers mainly to any trade unions that the employer recognizes and the right of the employee to join or not. It normally constitutes a statement of the specific terms and conditions by which both employer and employees are bound, and the specific procedures that are to be followed.

Discrimination and equality of opportunity

All organizations are required by law to be equal opportunity employers. It is illegal to discriminate between people when offering employment, promotion, pay, training and development or any other opportunity on all of the following grounds:

- racial or ethnic origin and religion;
- gender, including pregnancy, marital status and retirement age;
- disability (except where the employer's premises do not provide suitable access);
- membership of a trade union, refusal to join a trade union, insistence on joining or not joining a trade union;
- spent convictions for previous offences and misdemeanours (although there are many occupations exempted from this including teachers, doctors, lawyers, social workers, banking and finance).

Discrimination may be either direct or indirect. Direct discrimination is overt – the straightforward refusal of work or opportunities on any of the grounds indicated above. Indirect discrimination occurs where a condition or restraint is placed, the effect of which is to bar, restrict or jeopardize the opportunities of people from each of the groups indicated above.

Health and safety

An employer may not order or request an employee to carry out work that is hazardous or unsafe without first providing the correct protective equipment, clothing and training where necessary. An employer may not request, order or coerce an employee into carrying out any unsafe or hazardous activity.

It is the duty of employers to provide as far as reasonably practicable a healthy and safe working environment. It is the responsibility and duty of all to ensure that this is maintained and that accidents, hazards and emergencies are notified and rectified immediately.

Maternity

All female employees are entitled to 14 weeks' maternity leave regardless of length of service or hours worked. For those who have more than two years' continuous service the period is 29 weeks.

Pregnant employees are allowed time off with pay for ante-natal care.

On returning from maternity leave, the employee has the right to return to her previous job or (if this has ceased) to suitable alternative work.

Time off

Employers must allow reasonable time off from work for employees to carry out the following:

- public duties, including Justice of the Peace, members of local authorities, tribunals, health authorities, governorships of schools and colleges, boards of prison visitors; jury service if the employee is called;
- duties connected with the activities of recognized trade unions, including representation of members and training;
- looking for work and attending job interviews, retraining, career and occupational counselling after employees have been declared redundant and before they have left;
- maternity (as above).

Redundancy

Employers may dismiss – make redundant – employees whose work no longer exists or where fewer employees are required to carry out existing levels of work. Where redundancies are declared the employer must disclose the following:

- the reasons for the redundancies;
- the numbers and descriptions of employees affected;
- the criteria for selection;
- the means and dates on which the dismissals are to be carried out.

Employers must consult with any recognized trade unions as soon as it becomes known that redundancies are to occur. This must happen even if only one employee is to be made redundant.

Alternatives – short-time working, short-term lay-offs, transfers, redeployments, early retirements and calling for volunteers – must all be considered and rejected as impractical before compulsory redundancies take place.

The minimum consultation periods are as follows:

- 90 days in the case of 100 or more dismissals in a 90-day period;
- 30 days in the case of ten or more dismissals in a 30-day period;

otherwise consultation must begin as early as possible.

Employees who are dismissed because of redundancy are normally entitled to a lump sum payment. The amount depends on age, pay and length of service as follows.

For each year of continuous employment:

- from age 41–64, 1.5 weeks' pay
- from age 22–40, 1 week's pay
- from age 18–21, 0.5 week's pay.

In 1997, £205 is the maximum weekly pay that is taken into account and 20 years the maximum service. The maximum redundancy payment possible is therefore £6,150 (i.e. 20 years' service between 41 and 64 = 30 × 205).

The amount is reduced by one-twelfth for each month of service completed over the age of 64 so that at 65 (the statutory retirement age) no payment is due.

The employer must give the employee a written explanation of a redundancy payment.

Transfers of undertakings

The Transfer of Undertakings (Protection of Employment) regulations (TUPE) safeguard employees' rights when there is a change of employer following a change of ownership, takeover, merger or privatization. It also applies where there is a change of status – for example, from public to private sector, from building society to PLC.

The effects of the TUPE regulations are:

- The existing contract and terms and conditions of employment are transferred in their entirety to the new employer including continuity of service. The transfer may not take place with the purpose of reducing pay levels and other terms and conditions of employment.
- Recognition rights of trade unions are transferred if the new body maintains a distinctive identity.
- Dismissals related directly to the transfer of the business are automatically unfair.

- Both the old and the new employer must consult and provide advance information to any recognized trade unions and to all employees who are to be affected. This must include: the timing of the transfer; the reasons for the transfer; legal, economic and social implications for those affected.

Industrial action

Industrial action may be conducted in the pursuit of a legitimate trade dispute. A trade dispute occurs between employer and employees on one or more of the following grounds:

- Terms and conditions of employment.
- The physical conditions in which people are required to work.
- Dismissal, termination or suspension of employment of one or more employees.
- Allocation of work or duties.
- Matters of discipline.
- Membership or non-membership of a trade union.
- Facilities for officials of trade unions.
- Machinery for negotiation or consultation and other procedures relating to any of the above matters including the recognition by employers or employers' associations of the right of a trade union to represent employees.

Industrial action must be preceded by a postal ballot independently scrutinized (for example, by the electoral reform society). Those responsible for conducting a ballot (normally a trade union or staff representative) must give seven days notice of their intent to hold a ballot. They must notify the employer of the outcome and give seven days notice of any industrial action intended.

Payment

Payment must be made at the intervals stated in the contract and this must consist of the amounts stipulated.

Itemized pay statements must be issued at each interval. These must show the gross pay, the net pay, and the amount of each and every deduction made.

Individual rights

Individual rights at places of work have been clarified and strengthened over recent years. This has been partly due to UK government legislation and partly due to the European Union (EU). The main individual rights are:

- The right to fair and equal treatment regardless of length of service, hours worked or whether designated a full- or part-time employee.
- The right to employment protection (protection from unfair dismissal) after two years' continuous service regardless of hours worked or whether designated a full- or part-time employee.
- The right to join a recognized trade union or to refuse to join it; the right not to be penalized, victimized or harassed for joining or refusing to join.
- The right to adequate and continuous vocational and job training. The right to a healthy and safe working environment.
- The right to information, consultation and participation on key workplace issues and other matters of relevance and importance.
- The right of access to personnel files and other information held (whether on paper or database).
- The right to be represented or accompanied in all dealings with the organization, especially matters of grievance or discipline.

Notes

1 The great majority of applications made to an industrial tribunal are by individual employees. The orientation of the tribunal is therefore towards the individual. Where there is any doubt over the merits and strengths of the case of applicants and respondents, the tribunal normally orders the case to proceed.

2 Where there is any question that any of the rights indicated above have either been breached or not upheld, the tribunal will normally order the case to proceed.

3 It is the employer's duty to uphold the rights of individuals. The onus is therefore placed on the employer to be able to prove or demonstrate to the satisfaction of the tribunal that individual rights were upheld. It is the employer's duty to ensure that all employees are informed of their rights.

4 Employees may not be induced or coerced to sign away all or part of their statutory rights, nor is any such signature legally binding.

Recent cases that have acquired legal status and set precedent are as follows.

CASE EXAMPLES

Polkey v. A. E. Dayton Ltd

Organizations must follow procedures when dismissing an employee' Lords).

The ruling was as follows.

- In a case of incapacity an employee must be given fair warning and a chance to improve.
- In a case of misconduct, investigating fully and fairly and hearing what the employee has to say in explanation or mitigation of their conduct.
- In a case of redundancy, warning and consultation with affected employees and adopting a fair basis for selection and taking reasonable steps to redeploy those affected.

The tribunal which considered Polkey's case held that the employer had breached the correct procedure but that the result would have been the same if the procedure had been followed. This was rejected by the House of Lords.

The Lord Chancellor stated: 'It is what the employer did that is to be judged, not what he might have done.'

Heywood v. Cammell Laird

'Equal pay means pay and not equivalent benefits' (Lords).

Jean Heywood worked as a cook at Cammell Laird. For this work she was required to have a recognized qualification. She argued that her qualification was of the same level as those of men working elsewhere in the company and that therefore, her work was equivalent to that of those men. She was paid less than those men.

The company acknowledged that they paid Mrs Heywood less, but because she received a free meal every day this made her total reward package up to a level equivalent to that of the men with whom she was making the comparison.

The House of Lords rejected this and ordered the company to make up her pay to the same level as that of the men.

Brown v. Stockton-on-Tees Borough Council

'Pregnancy may not be used as a criterion for redundancy' (Lords).

Maria Brown worked for Stockton-on-Tees Borough Council. She worked in a group of four female staff. The Council made two members of staff redundant and singled Mrs Brown out as one of them because she was pregnant. If 'last in first out' had been used to determine redundancies. Mrs Brown would not have been made redundant: no other criteria for redundancy was published.

The Lords upheld the view that pregnancy was not a valid ground for redundancy; and that to make someone redundant because of their pregnancy amounted to discrimination. The Lords went on to state that criteria for redundancy must be published in advance of redundancies; failure to do so means that last in first out (lifo) will apply.

Price v. The Civil Service Commission

'Age constraints must not be indirectly discriminatory on grounds of gender' (Court of Appeal).

Belinda Price worked as a civil servant and, at the age of 36, put in for a promotion to the next grade. The Civil Service Commission turned her down on the grounds that she was too old and that everyone who made the particular grade had to do so by the age of 29. Ms Price countered this by saying that she could not have achieved this because she was out of the workforce for ten years bringing up children. She was otherwise a good and effective worker; the only thing militating against her promotion was her age; and that because of circumstances, this discriminated indirectly on grounds of gender.

The Court of Appeal upheld this view, stating that the particular age barrier was less favourable to women (and therefore discriminatory) than to men.

Burchell v. British Home Stores

'Allegations of misconduct must be fully investigated before any action is taken against an employee and before an employer comes to a decision as to what is to happen' (Court of Appeal).

Burchell was dismissed for misconduct by British Home Stores without being given the opportunity to state his case. The Court of Appeal laid down three guiding principles to ensure that natural justice would be upheld:

*   The employer should show that there was a genuine belief that the employee was guilty of the misconduct under consideration.
*   The employer must carry out a reasonable and thorough investigation into the case.
*   As the result of the investigation, the employer must have reasonable grounds for maintaining the belief.

Each point is now always considered and questioned by tribunals where cases arising from misconduct occur.

The following judgements were issued by The European Court of Justice after they had exhausted the tribunal and UK legal systems.

EUROPEAN COURT OF JUSTICE

Swift v. British Rail

'Retirement age and the opportunity to retire must be the same for all employees regardless of gender.'

British Rail v. National Union of Railwaymen

'Union membership agreements – the closed shop – are illegal and may not be enforced; no one should be forced to join a trade union or any other organization against their will nor should they be prevented from joining a trade union or any other organization if they so wish.'

PROCEDURES

Procedures exist to set standards of performance, conduct and behaviour at places of work and to ensure that everyone knows what is expected of them and that they conform to this. They ensure fairness and equality of treatment for everyone.

All organizations must have procedures for handling and managing discipline, grievance, disputes and dismissal. These have to meet standards prescribed by ACAS and the Department for Employment. They must:

- be in writing;
- state to whom they apply;
- be applied evenly to everyone concerned regardless of rank or occupation;
- be accessible, available for inspection and available for use at any time;
- be capable of being understood and followed;
- be fair and reasonable;
- indicate the disciplinary actions which may be taken in given sets of circumstances;
- indicate the levels of management which may take particular actions;
- provide for matters to be dealt with quickly.

DISCIPLINE

Disciplinary procedures must always include the following.

General rights

- The right of the individual to know the case against them and to confront their accuser.
- The right to respond to the case and present their own point of view.
- The right to representation at each stage, either by the representative of a recognized trade union or other person of their choice.
- The right to receive in writing a definitive statement of the conclusion and outcome of the case at each stage.
- The right of appeal against the conclusion and outcome at each stage.

Offences

Offences normally fall into the following categories.

- Minor offences and misdemeanours.
- Repetition of minor offences and misdemeanours.
- Serious misconduct.
- Gross misconduct.

The nature of each varies between organizations. Organizations must normally indicate the kind of offences that fall into each category.

Warnings

Minimum standards require for a series of at least two warnings (and many organizations have three or four). These may either be written or oral; when oral they are in any case normally confirmed in writing.

The general aim is to ensure that the employee is aware that an aspect of their conduct, behaviour or performance is unacceptable and giving cause for concern. The warning must confirm this and state the remedial action that is necessary.

For poor performance this normally includes retraining or a restatement of the standards of activity that are necessary and acceptable.

For shortfalls in behaviour and conduct this normally includes a restatement of what the required standards are and why they are necessary.

For both performance and conduct, warnings will normally include a date in the future on which a review of progress is to be carried out.

Recording

Warnings are recorded on the individual's personnel file (or equivalent) for set periods of time. Time periods are stated in the procedure and notified to the individual in each case.

It is normal for warnings for minor offences to be kept on file for periods of between three months and two years. Records of more serious offences may be retained for longer periods. The most serious offences are kept on file for life.

There are no rules governing this. The only requirement is to be fair and reasonable. The organization must balance its need to set and maintain standards with the requirement of individuals not to have their career or their prospects irreparably harmed by relatively minor incidents.

At the end of the stated period, the warning is removed from the file. It may never be used or referred to again.

Serious misconduct

For matters of serious misconduct it is acceptable and legitimate to place individuals on a final warning. This is confirmed to the individual in writing as the result of the hearing and assessment of the case.

Organizations must indicate the kind of offences that constitute serious misconduct (though the list need not be exhaustive). These normally include persistent bad time-keeping, persistent poor performance, rudeness and insubordination.

Gross misconduct

For gross misconduct it is acceptable and legitimate to move straight to dismissal. This is normally called summary dismissal. This is also confirmed to the individual in writing as the result of the hearing and assessment of the case.

Organizations must again indicate the kind of offences that constitute gross misconduct (though the list again need not be exhaustive). These normally include vandalism, violence, arson, sabotage, theft, dishonesty, sexual misconduct, sale and publication of confidential information, other breaches of the criminal law, and harassment, persecution and victimization of members of staff.

For both serious misconduct and gross misconduct, procedures must be followed. However serious the alleged offence, the individual is still entitled to hear the case against them, to face their accuser, to respond, to be represented and to appeal against the findings.

Where dismissal does occur the reasons stated for dismissal must be the real reason for dismissal. This must be notified in writing to the individual and to anyone else who requests the information (for example, the Department of Social Security).

Suspension

For serious offences it is acceptable and legitimate to suspend employees from work while a full investigation into the matter is held. Suspension is normally on full pay. The reasons for suspension and the date and time from which it becomes effective must be confirmed in writing at the point at which the decision to suspend is made.

Disciplinary hearings

For all disciplinary hearings the employee must be informed of the following:

- They must be notified, either orally or in writing, that they are required to attend a disciplinary hearing. The words 'disciplinary hearing' must be used. They must be informed of all the rights indicated above, including the right to be accompanied and represented.

- They must be informed of the case against them, who has brought it and why. They must be given the opportunity to face their accuser. They must be informed of the nature of the case, whether it potentially constitutes a minor offence, repeat offence, serious misconduct or gross misconduct.
- They must be asked to give their explanation of the events and situation.
- They must be allowed time (but not excessive) to prepare their case. They must be allowed to call witnesses and gain access to documents and papers that affect their case.

All employees have the right to raise issues, concerns and problems with their employer. This normally consists of: **GRIEVANCE**

- Raising the matter with the immediate supervisor, either informally or formally.
- If there is no satisfaction, raising the matter with the next level of management.
- If there is still no satisfaction, raising the matter with upper levels of management including ultimate reference to the chair, managing director, chief executive officer or equivalent.
- The right to have present a witness or observer and to be represented.
- The right to appeal against the proposed resolution if this is felt not to be satisfactory. The right to receive the outcome or resolution in writing.

Most issues are resolved to the satisfaction of everyone at the initial stage. The rest exists to ensure that serious matters – especially victimization or discrimination – can be fully and adequately dealt with.

There is an exception to this. Where the employer has fewer than 20 employees, formal grievance procedures are not required. However, employees must be told the name of the person who should be approached if they have a grievance or concern.

Complete up-to-date records constantly maintained are essential. They must include copies of the contract of employment and other terms and conditions. They must also include copies of all formal communications between employer and employee, and especially notes of warnings, conduct, behaviour and performance. Other documentation is also useful, especially general notes, file notes, diary entries, records and minutes of meetings, performance appraisal statements and other general features.   **PERSONNEL RECORDS**

The purpose is to provide an accurate and truthful record of the period of employment. This material is also invariably both useful and required if the employee does at some stage make a complaint at a tribunal.

SOURCES OF
INFORMATION

Expert bodies

Advisory, Conciliation and Arbitration Service (ACAS)

ACAS is an independent statutory body funded by government grant. It is the recognized national source of expertise, advice, information and guidance on workplace industrial relations and staff management. ACAS publishes guidelines and codes of practice on discipline, grievance, dismissal, employment practices and the content and use of procedures. These are available from offices of ACAS, either free or for a small charge.

The general role of ACAS is to promote workplace harmony, understanding and well-being.

*   *Advice:* ACAS may be contacted at any time, either by post or phone on any aspect of workplace, industrial relations or staff management for general advice and information. ACAS officials also arrange and carry out briefings and training sessions by agreement.
*   *Conciliation and mediation:* ACAS may be contacted at any time to arrange conciliation and mediation in disputes that are likely to become serious if they are not resolved quickly. ACAS searches for common grounds and areas where agreement might be reached and makes proposals for tackling other issues. ACAS also conducts conciliation and mediation in all applications to tribunal as stated above.
*   *Arbitration:* ACAS may be contacted at any time to arrange arbitration in disputes where there is no apparent possibility of resolution. Both parties normally agree to be bound by the arbitrator's findings (though this is not required by law). The arbitrator hears both cases and then makes recommendations based on their assessment of the merits. The result may be wholly in favour of one party or a compromise between the two, or some alternative solution.

In all cases that come to hearing, the tribunal normally requires satisfaction that the advice, proposals, recommendations and guidance of ACAS have been followed. Where this has not occurred, good reasons must be shown. Where both parties agree to be bound by the findings of an arbitrator, good reason must be shown if one party then decides not to accept these findings.

Health and Safety Executive (HSE)

HSE is also an independent body funded by government grant. It is the recognized source of expertise, advice, information and guidance on all matters concerning health and safety at work.

The HSE publishes advice and guidelines on general health and safety matters. It has a statutory right of access to all work premises. It carries out inspections, advises on safety matters, and in extreme cases may close down premises or parts of premises where these are considered to be unsafe or unhealthy.

Where a case arises from health and safety matters the tribunal always requires satisfaction that the advice, proposals, recommendations and guidance of the HSE has been followed. If this has not occurred, good reason must be shown.

Department for Employment (DE)

The DE publishes booklets and leaflets giving advice and information on changes to the law and the implementation of regulations. It is the duty of employers to ensure that they keep themselves up-to-date with current employment legislation.

A tribunal never accepts ignorance of the law as a defence – whether on the part of applicant or respondent.

Commission for Racial Equality, Equal Opportunities Commission, Disablement Resettlement Officer

These bodies provide independent advice and guidance, and act as a source of information on employment law and related matters. Their advice and guidance is normally considered to be the highest form of expertise available.

In tribunal cases where the advice and guidance of these bodies has been sought, the tribunal will normally place great emphasis on their recommendations.

Trade Unions, Employers' Associations, Professional Associations, Independent Associations

These bodies provide advice and guidance and act as a source of information on employment law and related matters to their members. Their advice and guidance carries no particular presumption of expertise. It is, however, generally of high quality and represents the state of knowledge and information available.

Tribunals may choose to place emphasis on the recommendations, advice and guidance given by these bodies.

Laws and regulations

The main laws, and their coverage, are as follows.

Equal Pay Act 1970

- *Equal pay:* the right to receive the same pay and other terms of employment as an employee of the opposite sex working for the same or an associated employer if engaged on like work, work rated as equivalent or work of equal value.

Employment Protection (Consolidation) Act 1978

- *Pay:* the right to receive an itemized pay statement.
- *Maternity rights:* the right not to be unfairly dismissed for reasons connected with pregnancy; the right to paid time off work for ante-natal care; the right to return to work following absence because of pregnancy or confinement.
- *Medical suspension:* the right not to be unfairly dismissed on medical grounds; the right to receive pay for suspension on medical grounds.
- *Redundancy:* the right to be consulted by the employer about proposed redundancies; the right of recognized independent trade unions to be consulted by the employer about proposed redundancies; the right to receive payment when made redundant; the right to receive an itemized statement of redundancy payment; the right to pay and time off in the event of redundancy to look for other work or to make arrangements for training.
- *Time off for public duties:* the right to time off for public duties.
- *Trade union membership/non-membership rights:* the right to pay and time off for trade union duties; the right to time off for trade union activities; the right not to suffer dismissal or action short of dismissal for trade union membership or activities or non-membership; the right not to suffer action short of dismissal to compel union membership; the right not to be unfairly dismissed for trade union membership or activities; the right not to be unfairly dismissed for non-membership of the union; the right not to be chosen for redundancy because of trade union membership or activities, or non-membership of a trade union.
- *Unfair dismissal:* the right not to be unfairly dismissed for any reason; the right to receive a written statement of reasons for dismissal; the right to receive a written statement of terms of employment and any alterations to them.

Race Relations Act 1976

- *Race relations:* the right not to be discriminated against in employment, training and related fields on grounds of colour, race, nationality, ethnic or national origin.

Sex Discrimination Act 1975

- *Sex discrimination:* the right not to be discriminated against in employment, training and related fields on the grounds of sex, marriage or pregnancy.

Transfer of Undertakings (Protection of Employment) Regulations 1981

- *Transfers:* the right of unions to be informed and consulted about the transfer of an undertaking to a new employer; the right not to be dismissed on the transfer of an undertaking to a new employer.

Employment Act 1980

- *Trade union rights:* the right not to be unreasonably excluded or expelled from a trade union.

Employment Act 1988

- *Trade union rights:* the right not to be unjustifiably disciplined by a trade union; the right of recourse to a tribunal if discriminated or disciplined by an employer concerning trade union rights; the right of trade unions to hold secret ballots on employer's premises.

Wages Act 1961

- *Payment of wages:* the right of all staff not to have deductions made from their wages unless allowed by statute by the contract of employment or with the individual's prior written agreement; the right of everyone to an itemized pay statement.

Disabled Persons (Employment) Acts 1944, 1958 and 1996

- *Disability:* the general right not to be discriminated against in employment because of a registered disability; the duty of employers with 20 or more employees to employ a minimum of 3% of registered disabled people; the right to complain to tribunal if discriminated against or disadvantaged by virtue of disability.

Rehabilitation of Offenders Act 1971

- *Spent convictions:* job applicants and employees are not under any legal obligation to disclose information about previous convictions; the right to deny a previous offence when the conviction for it is 'spent' – a person has served their punishment and been rehabilitated (there are a large number of occupations which are exempted from this rule – especially working with money, people and property; and working within the legal, law enforcement and emergency services).

Trade Union Reform and Employment Rights Act 1993

- *Employee rights:* the right not to be dismissed for exercising statutory employment rights regardless of length of service or hours of work; the right of women to 14 weeks' maternity leave regardless of length of service or hours of work; the right to healthy and safe working premises and activities regardless of length of service or hours of work.
- *Transfers of undertakings:* the regulations governing business transfers are extended to cover non-commercial undertakings.
- *Trade unions:* individuals are given the right to join the union of their choice; the deduction of union dues from pay must be authorized in writing by the employees every three years; the duty of an employer to inform and consult union representatives about collective redundancies is re-stated.
- *Industrial action:* strike ballots must be postal and independently scrutinized; unions must give employers seven days' notice of their intention to hold a strike ballot; unions must give employers seven days' notice of the industrial action intended; injunctions may be sought by anybody affected by unlawful or unofficial industrial action to prevent this from taking place.

European Union law

European Union law is broadly superior to UK law; any case that reaches the European Court of Justice will be judged by this as the final conclusion to the matter in hand. The particular concern of European Union law is the strengthening and upholding of individual rights in all aspects of life – and this includes employment. The main areas of concern are:

- *Freedom of movement* for workers and self-employed persons across the European Union.
- *Protection of employment and remuneration;* adequate vocational training.
- *Freedom of association,* especially the right to join trade unions and associations, or not to join trade unions and associations.
- *Information consultation and participation* of employees on major workplace issues.
- *Health and safety* at work.
- Specific *protection for stated groups of employees,* especially children, adolescents, elderly persons, disabled persons; equal treatment for men and women.

The general principle is that current UK legislation reflects the demands of EU law and standards. It is especially important to note that any case that does reach the European Court of Justice will be judged by persons who take a European perspective.

Appendix B

The European Community Social Charter

Freedom of Movement

Every worker of the European Community shall have the right to freedom of movement throughout the territory of the Community subject to restrictions justified on grounds of public order, public safety or public health. The right to freedom of movement shall enable to engage in any occupation or profession in the Community in accordance with the principles of equal treatment as regards access to employment, working conditions and social protection in the host country. The rights of freedom of movement shall also imply:

- harmonization of conditions of residence in all Member States, particularly those concerning family reunifications;
- elimination of obstacles arising from the non-recognition of diplomas or equivalent occupational qualifications;
- improvement of the living and working conditions of frontier workers.

Employment and remuneration

Every individual shall be free to choose and engage in an occupation according to the regulations governing each occupation. All employment shall be fairly remunerated. To this effect in accordance with arrangements applying in each country:

- workers shall be assured of an equitable wage, that is, a wage sufficient to enable them to have a decent standard of living;
- workers subject to terms of employment other than an open-ended full-time contract shall receive an equitable reference wage;
- wages may be withheld, seized or transferred only in accordance with the provisions of national law; such provisions should entail measures enabling the worker concerned to continue to enjoy the necessary means of subsistence for themselves and their families.

Every individual must be able to access to public placement services free of charge.

FUNDAMENTAL SOCIAL RIGHTS OF WORKERS

Improvement of living and working conditions

The completion of the internal market must lead to an improvement in the living and working conditions of workers in the European Community. This process must result from an approximation of these conditions while the improvement is being maintained as regards in particular to duration and organization of working time and forms of employment other than open-ended contracts such as fixed-term contracts, part-time working, temporary work and seasonal work.

This improvement must cover where necessary the developments of certain aspects of employment regulations such as procedures for collective redundancies and those regarding bankruptcies.

Every worker of the European Community shall have a right to a weekly rest period and annual paid leave, the duration of which must be harmonized in accordance with national practices while the improvement is being maintained.

The conditions of employment of every worker of the European Community shall be stipulated in laws in a collective agreement or in a contract of employment according to arrangements applying in each country.

Social protection

Every worker of the European Community shall have a right to adequate social protection and shall whatever their status and whatever the size of the undertaking in which they are employed enjoy an adequate level of social security benefits.

Persons who have been unable either to enter or re-enter the labour market and have no means of subsistence must be able to receive sufficient resources and social assistance in keeping with their particular situation.

Freedom of association

Employers and workers of the European Community shall have the right of association in order to constitute professional organizations or trade unions of their choice for the defence of their economic and social interests.

Every employer and every worker shall have the freedom to join or not to join such organizations without any personal or occupational damage being suffered by him.

Employers or employers' organizations on the one hand and workers' organizations on the other shall have the right to negotiate and conclude collective agreements under the conditions laid down by national legislation and practice. The dialogue between the two sides of industry at European level which must be developed may, if the party deem it desirable, result in contractual relations in particular at inter-occupational and sectoral level.

The right to resort to collective action in the event of a conflict of interest shall include the right to strike subject to the obligations arising under national regulations and collective agreements. In order to facilitate the settlement of industrial disputes the establishment and utilization at the appropriate level of conciliation, mediation and arbitration procedures should be encouraged in accordance with national practice.

The internal legal order of the Member States shall determine under which conditions and to what extent the rights provided in Articles 11 to 13 apply to armed forces, the police and civil services.

Vocational training

Every worker of the European Community must be able to have access to vocational training and to receive such training throughout their working life. In the conditions governing access to such training there may be no discrimination on grounds of nationality. The competent public authorities undertakings or the two sides of industry each within their own sphere of competence, should set up continuing and permanent training systems enabling every person to undergo retraining, more especially to relieve the training purposes to improve the skills or to acquire new skills particularly in the light of technical developments.

Equality treatment for men and women

Equal treatment for men and women must be assured. Equal opportunities for men and women must be developed. To this end action should be intensified wherever necessary to ensure the implementation of the principle of equality between men and women as regards in particular access to employment, remuneration, working conditions, social protection, education, vocational training and career development. Measures should also be developed enabling men and women to reconcile their occupational and family obligations.

Information, consultation and participation for workers

Information, consultation and participation for workers must be developed along appropriate lines, taking account of the practices in force in various Member States. This shall apply especially in companies or groups of companies having establishments or companies in several Member States of the European Community.

Such information, consultation and participation must be implemented in due time, particularly in the following cases:

- when technological changes which from the point of view of working conditions and work organizations have major implications for the workforce are introduced into undertakings;
- in connection with restructuring operations in undertakings or in cases of mergers having an impact on the employment of workers;
- in cases of collective redundancy procedures;
- when trans-frontier workers in particular are affected by employment policies pursued by the undertaking where they are employed.

Health, protection and safety at the workplace

Every worker must enjoy satisfactory health and safety conditions in his working environment. Appropriate measures must be taken in order to achieve further harmonization and conditions in this area while maintaining the improvements made. These measures shall take account in particular of the need for training, information, consultation and balanced participation of workers as regard to the risks incurred and the steps taken to eliminate or reduce them. The provisions regarding implementation of the internal market shall help ensure such protection.

Protection of children and adolescents

Without prejudice to such rules as may be more favourable to young people – in particular those ensuring their preparation for work through vocational training and subject to derogations limited to certain light work, the minimum employment age must not be lower than the minimum school-leaving age and, in any case, not lower than 15 years.

Young people who are in gainful employment must receive equitable remuneration in accordance with national practice. Appropriate measures must be taken to adjust labour regulations applicable to young workers so that their specific needs regarding development, vocational training and access to employment are met.

The duration of work must in particular be limited – without it being possible to circumvent this limitation through recourse to overtime – and night work prohibited in the case of workers under 18 years of age except in certain jobs laid down in national legislation or regulations.

Following the end of compulsory education young people must be entitled to receive initial vocational training of a sufficient duration to enable them to adapt to the requirements of their future working life: for young workers such training should take place during working hours.

Elderly persons

According to the arrangements applying in each country every worker of the European Community must, at the time of retirement, be able to enjoy resources affording them a decent standard of living.

Every person who has reached retirement but who is not entitled to a pension or who does not have other means of subsistence must be entitled to sufficient resources and to medical and social assistance specifically suited to their needs.

Disabled persons

All disabled persons, whatever the origin and nature of disablement, must be entitled to additional concrete measures aimed at improving their social and professional integration. These measures must concern in particular according to the capacities of the beneficiaries, vocational training, ergonomics, accessibility, mobility, means of transport and housing.

Implementation of the Charter

It is more particularly the responsibility of the Member States in accordance with national practices, notably through legislative measures or collective agreements, to guarantee the fundamental social rights in this Charter and to implement the social measures indispensable to the smooth operation of the internal market as part of a strategy of economic and social cohesion.

The European Council invites the Commission to submit as soon as possible initiatives which fall within its powers as provided for in the Treaties with a view to the adoption of legal instruments for the effective implementation as and when the internal market is completed of those rights which come within the Community's area of competence.

The Commission shall establish each year during the last three months, a report on the application of the Charter by the Member States and by the European Community.

The report of the Commission shall be forwarded to the European Council, the European Parliament and the Economic and Social Committee.

In summary the content of the Charter is as follows:

- The freedom of movement for workers and self-employed persons across the EC.
- Adequate provisions for employment and remuneration.
- Improvement of living and working conditions.
- Adequate social protection and social security.
- Freedom of association and the right to join or not join trade unions and associations.
- Vocational training.
- Equal treatment for men and women.
- Information, consultation and participation of workers on key workplace issues.

- Health, safety and welfare at work.
- Protection of children and adolescents at work.
- Protection for the elderly.
- Access for the disabled to labour markets and protection of disabled persons.

By the Treaty of Rome and the Treaty of Maastricht, EC law is superior to UK law where the same topics are covered. EC Articles of law are binding on all employers immediately. EC Directives are binding on all governments and public services. They are also strongly influential in all relevant case law. Non-statutory and non-binding instruments (in particular recommendations) are nevertheless strongly evidential.

The status of the United Kingdom is that it has secured for itself an opt-out from the implementation of the Social Charter. The status and influence of this opt-out is uncertain.

Appendix C

Glossary

ACAS The Advisory, Conciliation and Arbitration Service. ACAS provides advice and guidance on all matters of employment and may be called upon to intervene in disputes and problems. ACAS may be contacted at any time on any general employment matter.

BS 5750/ISO 9000 The Award of the British Standards Institute (BSI) for total quality management, and high levels of commitment to staff and customers.

Career break The practice of offering extended periods of leave to staff after a certain period of employment. This normally takes the form either of a sabbatical (in which the employee is free to do whatever they choose during the career break), or for child care. Those who take career breaks are given full continuity of employment when they return to work.

Conformism The setting of distinctive patterns of attitudes and behaviour to which all employees are required to agree.

Contract of Employment The formalization of the working relationship between employer and employee.

Contract for services The formalization of the working relationship between one organization and another – e.g. a subcontractor, an agency.

Core and peripheral workforce The core is the permanent workforce; the peripheral is made up of those parts of the workforce which are hired and employed at specific times or for particular purposes.

Corporate culture The combination of organizational activities, behaviour and attitudes – 'the way things are done'.

Counselling The practice of giving personal support to members of staff in difficulty, with problems, or any general matter of employment.

Custom and practice The work patterns and activities which grow up as a matter of habit over a period of time.

Data Protection Act 1988 The law that governs what may be held on file about employees. Any information that is held about employees must be made available to them (this includes both paper and electronic files).

Discrimination Practice of differentiating between people on particular grounds. Discrimination may be lawful – differentiating on grounds of capability or attitude; or unlawful – discriminating on grounds of race, gender, marital status, membership or not of a trade union etc.

Employment Department The Employment Department of the Department for Education and Employment issues guidelines and advice to employers on all aspects of working.

Employment protection The legal protection from bullying, victimization, harassment or discrimination at all times; protection from unfair dismissal – i.e. dismissal for no good reason, or when procedures have not been followed – for all employees after two years' service.

Employment Protection Consolidation Act 1987 (EPCA) The main law that governs the Contract of Employment and other aspects of the working relationship.

Empowerment The practice of giving individual employees responsibility, autonomy and authority over the nature and quality of their work.

Equality The principle on which all employees are treated.

Flexible benefits Rewards and advantages gained by employees as the result of working for the particular organization, and to which they may subscribe if they so choose.

Full-time and part-time working The description of the traditional work pattern of the UK; as the result of flexible working and changes in employment legislation, the distinction has become blurred. For best practice and best results, full-time and part-time employees are treated the same.

Genuine Occupational Qualification (GOQ) Any skill or quality required of an individual to do a particular job. A GOQ is the only reason why any form of race, gender or disability discrimination may occur.

Health and Safety at Work Act 1974 (HASAWA) The legislation governing all matters of health and safety at work in the UK.

Home-working The practice of having people working from their homes rather than from organizational premises.

Implied terms Those matters not stated in a Contract of Employment, but which may reasonably be expected to apply.

Incentive schemes The practice of offering additional rewards for successful and effective work.

Induction The practice of settling people into their place of work; the practice of instilling the required standards, attitudes and behaviour at the outset of employment.

Investors In People (IIP) An award made by governments to employers confirming the employer's commitment to its workforce.

Job description A statement of tasks and activities to be carried out by the job holder.

Job enrichment The practice of extending and enlarging the quality and volume of work to be carried out by an individual.

Job share The practice of dividing up a full-time job between two or three employees (job sharers).

Just in time The ability to call up staff, supplies, components and equipment at short notice whenever they are required.

Labour costs The total cost of employing people. Labour costs always include salary, national insurance, pension, equipment, accommodation, heating and lighting; some employers also include supervision, training, down/unproductive time, other benefits and rewards. It is usual to regard labour costs as fixed costs (rather than variable costs).

Labour/employee/industrial relations The regulation of activities, behaviour and attitudes that exist at places of work; systems and procedures for the resolution of conflict, the behavioural aspects of staff management.

Managing by Walking About (MBWA) A term used to describe highly visible and personal styles of supervision.

Maternity rights The legal requirement to give all female employees 14 weeks' maternity leave regardless of length of service or hours worked; the legal requirement to give female employees up to 29 weeks' maternity leave after two years' continuous service: the requirement to give all pregnant female employees reasonable time off to attend pre-natal health checks and care.

Organization Development (OD) Organizational commitment to continuous improvement in all areas; commitment to continuous staff training; commitment to job and work enlargement; commitment to streamlining and simplification of procedures.

Person specification The statement of qualities and attributes required of a person to do a particular job. This normally mirrors the job description.

Premium rates/eonomic rent The need to make high levels of pay and reward for certain types of work; the ability to demand high rates of pay and reward for certain types of work.

Quality of working life The creation of effective and successful work environments, in which high and successful levels of output can be achieved.

Recognition The relationship between employers and their trade unions; all employers have the right to recognize or not to recognize trade unions.

Rostering The practice of organizing staff into distinctive work patterns.

Seven-point plan A form of person specification.

Shift patterns The organization of people into regular times of work. Term-time working, the practice of employing people to work during school term times and requiring them to take substantial periods of leave during the school holidays. Continuity of employment is normally guaranteed.

Telecommuting The practice of 'commuting', locking into working systems, maintaining a working relationship between employer and employee, through the use of electronic supervision systems, e-mail, and other information technology.

Teleconferencing The practice of holding meetings and conferences through the telephone network, supported by someone at the centre of the meeting having a multi-audio facility.

Testing for employability The practice of requiring potential employees to take tests that indicate their ability, aptitude, potential or attitude for and towards particular types of work.

Total Quality Management (TQM) An approach to organization management based on product, service and working life quality.

Trade union A national institution whose objectives are to represent the best interests of their members in places of work.

Trade Union Reform and Employment Rights Act 1993 (TURERA) The employment legislation that guarantees minimum maternity rights; and employment protection to all members of staff regardless of whether full-time or part-time.

Transfer of Undertakings Protection of Employment (TUPE) Regulation The regulations that guarantee continuity of employment and protection of terms and conditions of employment (including pay) at the time when ownership of an organization or function is changed.

Bibliography

M. K. Ash (1985) *On People Management*, MacDonald.

R. Cartwright *et al.* (1994) *Management*, Blackwell.

A. Chattell (1995) *Managing for the Future*, Macmillan.

P. F. Drucker (1993) *The Post Capitalist Society*, HarperCollins.

W. Goldsmith & D. Clutterbuck (1990) *The Winning Streak*, Penguin.

J. H. Goldthorpe *et al.* (1968) *The Affluent Worker*, Vols. I, II and III, Cambridge University Press.

J. Harvey-Jones (1990) *Making it Happen*, Fontana.

F. Herzberg (1974) *Work and the Nature of Man*, Granada.

R. M. Kanter (1985) *When Giants Learn to Dance*, Free Press.

R. M. Kanter (1990) *The Change Masters*, Free Press.

R. S. Lessem (1987) *Intrapreneurship*, Wildwood.

R. Likert (1961) *New Patterns of Management*, McGraw-Hill.

M. H. McCormack (1989) *Success Secrets*, Fontana.

A. H. Maslow (1987) *Motivation and Personality*, Harper & Row.

A. Morita (1987) *Made in Japan: The Sony Story*, Fontana.

R. Pascale & A. Athos (1983) *The Art of Japanese Management*, Fontana.

T. Peters & N. Austin (1985) *A Passion for Excellence*, Collins.

R. Pettinger (1997) *Introduction to Management*, Macmillan.

R. Pettinger & R. Frith (1996) *Managing the Flexible Workforce*, Technical Communications.

R. Pettinger & R. Frith (1996) *Measuring Business and Managerial Performance*, STC.

J. Rice (1995) *Doing Business in Japan*, Penguin.

A. Roddick (1992) *Body and Soul: The Body Shop Story*, Ebury.

R. Semler (1992) *Maverick*, Free Press.

R. Stewart (1991) *Managing Today and Tomorrow*, Macmillan.

E. Sternberg (1995) *Just Business*, Warner.

M. Trevor (1992) *Toshiba's New British Company*, Policy Studies Institute.

V. Vroom & E. L. Deci (1992) *Management and Motivation*, Penguin.

A. Williams & P. Dobson (1995) *Changing Culture*, IPD.

Index